THE NEW MATH SAT GAME PLAN

The Strategic Way to Score Higher

Philip Keller

The New Math SAT Game Plan

www.satgameplan.com

ISBN 978-0-9815896-0-2

Please note:

This is not a math textbook. And it's not one of those phone-book-sized review books, either.

I actually expect you to <u>read</u> this book from cover to cover.

If you do, and if you follow the instructions, your SAT math score will go up.

Now start reading.

"Do you see how I got that problem right? It's all you-- I could hear your voice in my head: 'You just have to go a little slower, look a little deeper.' I actually <u>enjoyed</u> doing that problem."

-- Patrick C. (former student)

About the Author

Teaching SAT math has been Philip Keller's "other job" since 1985. While studying mechanical engineering at Princeton University, he taught SAT classes for a company called Pre-Test Review, a pioneer in SAT preparation. After graduating, he became a high school math and science teacher, teaching mostly physics but also chemistry, calculus and geometry. All through his years of teaching, he has continued to work with students to prepare them for the SAT.

He has also worked as a free-lance writer for the ACT, writing math and science questions, so he has seen the standardized testing world from inside and out. Currently, he teaches physics at Holmdel High School, in Holmdel, New Jersey. He also teaches the math classes for *Keller and White*, a small SAT and PSAT preparation program.

He lives in Shrewsbury, New Jersey, with his wife Daphne, his children Reuben and Jane, and his dogs, Ranger, Stella and Pippin.

Contents

7   Introduction: "Hey, Mr. Keller, you sound like an infomercial"

12   *Memo: About calculators*

13   PART I: "I say, you're going about it all wrong, son!"

17   Lesson #1: It's About <u>Time</u>

33   Lesson #2: No Algebra, Please…

41   Lesson #3: The Back Door Play

50   *Memo: The well-meant words that do you harm: "I'm not a good test-taker"*

53   Lesson #4: The Grid-ins

61   Lesson #5: "When should I guess?"

64   *Memo: Testing with Extended Time*

        Part II: Actual Math -- The Essential SAT Topics

67   Round 1 - Middle School Topics

97   Round 2 – Geometry Topics

127   Round 3 – Algebra II

151   Round 4 – Miscellaneous Fun Stuff that shows up on the SAT

175   One Last Word: What to expect on test day

177   Just For Teachers: How to use this book in your SAT course

INTRODUCTION

"Hey, Mr. Keller. You sound like an infomercial"

I know a secret about the SAT. Listen carefully.

There are many things in life that require patience and hard work. Many skills require years and years to learn. Many talented people find that they have to practice for a long time before they see improvement in their performance level, whether you are talking about playing golf, running a marathon, or playing the violin. No pain, no gain. You get out what you put in. Blah, blah, blah. OK, here comes the secret:

The math SAT is NOT ONE OF THOSE THINGS!

You will be surprised to see how easy it is to raise your score. But how can that be so? If there were an easy way, wouldn't everybody have heard about it by now? In this internet age of instant communication, how can there be a set of secret tricks that only a tiny percentage of test-takers ever find out about? I honestly have no idea! I think that kids should already know this stuff. But they don't. Time after time, I introduce my methods to students and I am met with astonishment, followed by relief, as one after another, they discover the easier way.

If you are like the vast majority of the students I have worked with, you have been attacking this test with the wrong strategy, using the wrong techniques, and badly mismanaging your time. These things are not hard to fix. And when you fix them, your score jumps up.

Then, you can review a small collection of math concepts and tricks that show up frequently on the SAT. After all, if even a half-dozen show up on your exam, and you have learned how to deal with them, then your score will take another upward jump.

And finally, you can take practice tests, where you apply your newfound knowledge and your new strategies and techniques. This way, you can monitor your progress as you practice what you have learned from this book. And as a result of all that practice, your score takes another jump.

I know these methods work. There are certain seasons of the year, shortly after the most recent SAT scores have been released, when I get the phone calls. Or students stop me in the hallway of the high school where I teach to give me their good news:

> *"Hey, thanks a lot. I went up 110 points in math."*
> *"Hey Mr. Keller, you were right. I got a 680".*
> *"Mr. Keller! I got an 800!"*
> *"I went from a 450 to a 580. Can I take your course again?"*

What most of these students are happiest about is how QUICKLY we accomplished this. The SAT course I teach meets for six sessions. It is unusual for me to work one-on-one with a student for more than 4 or 5 hours. Sometimes two or three hours is all it takes. In one extreme example, well, I'll quote the message that was left on my answering machine:

"Mr. Keller, I just want to thank you for taking the time to talk to my daughter. I know you only spoke to her for twenty minutes, but she did everything you said and her score went up 130 points."

I promise that's a true story. It is, of course, an extreme case, involving a student who was doing EVERYTHING wrong, but in a way that could quickly be adjusted. Like most students, she approached the SAT the way she learned to take tests in school. But when it comes to the SAT, the traditional school methods don't work for most students. Fortunately, there are non-traditional methods that DO work, methods that can be learned easily and quickly. It's not magic. It's not rocket science. It's not the miracle cure that you have seen on television. It's just that there is a better way to take this test, and when you learn it, you improve your score.

My first job is to convince you that it is possible to achieve a big increase quickly (but NOT effortlessly). I want you to have higher expectations. That's why sometimes I end up sounding like an infomercial. That's what I was told by one of my students on the first day of his SAT class. This student was actually kind of obnoxious. He wasn't too thrilled to be taking an SAT course and he was not the kind of student who always does what the teacher says. You could call him a non-conformist[*]. And he is precisely the kind of student I can help the most! After his SAT, he was just another one of those kids who thank me in the hall.

This just in: It happened AGAIN! I just got another phone call thanking me for the advice I gave over the phone. The student's score went up 190 points. I've never even met this kid. I just told her what to do over the phone. It really worked and it set my new record for largest, fastest improvement ever. This time, even I find it hard to believe. It's kind of spooky.

---

[*] You'll be hearing more about these non-conformists later. They tend to do well on the SAT, better in fact than their grades in school might lead you to expect. Meanwhile, hard-working, "good" students frequently "under score". It's important to learn why this happens and how to turn it to your advantage.

How to use this book: A guide for STUDENTS

(If you are a teacher, your guide is in the back of the book)

I have written this book to give my students a competitive advantage over the rest of the test-taking universe: I am going to help you raise your math score.

What _you_ will have to do:

1. Well, obviously you have to read each section.

2. You have to work through the samples in the section and I mean <u>actually work them out</u>. You should be reading this book with a pencil and a calculator by your side.

3. After each section, there is a short practice set of problems for you to apply what that section teaches. The answers and explanations are on the pages after each problem set.

PLEASE NOTE: The practice problems are, in general, more toward the difficult side. Do NOT worry if you need to peek at the answers. It's good to practice with harder questions. But it's also important to practice with the right level problem. And that is why…

4. You have to take practice tests. At different points throughout the book, I'll tell you that it is time to go do a practice test. Ideally, you should do three or four actual practice tests before taking the real SAT. And in this case, more is better. Six would be good.

Wait a minute! This is a pretty skinny book. I don't see practice tests anywhere. How am I supposed to practice?

Yes, it's true. There are no full-length practice tests in this book. It's not because I couldn't make them up -- I write tests all the time. It's because if I did, they would not be the real thing. And there is no point practicing with fake tests. Think about it: if you were playing in the Superbowl, and you needed to scout your opponents, wouldn't you want films of their actual games? Or would you settle for a bunch of players dressed up to look like your opponent? I think you'd want the real thing. Same is true here…you need <u>actual</u> SATs. Most of the books in the SAT section of the bookstore are filled with fake SATs written by recent college graduates, typeset to look very much like the real thing. (I know because I was once one of those recent graduates. At the time, I never imagined that I would one day write actual questions for the ACT.) But you have to remember that the books are not real, and the tests in them are misleading. They often include material that ETS never uses, they are not at the right level of difficulty and they take longer than they should. Don't use them. ONLY PRACTICE WITH ACTUAL SATS! There are several ways for you to get them.

1. You can probably get one sample exam in a booklet at your school's guidance office.

2. You can ask older brothers and sisters or older friends if they sent away for their exam (It's called the 'Question and Answer Service' and it's available several times a year).

3. You can buy a book, put out by the College Board, called The Official SAT Study Guide. It costs about $15. If I were you, I'd buy it. We use it in the class I teach and I tell anybody I tutor to get it right away. Ignore the entire first half of the book, which is filled with useless information, bad advice and half-truths. The practice tests begin somewhere in the middle.

.

How to Take a Practice Test

As you go through this book, you will see that I frequently compare the SAT to an athletic event. Partly, this is so I can use all the cool clichés that the coaches use. Here's one you may have heard once or twice: *You have to practice like you want to play.*

In this case, what that means is that when you take a practice test, you need to:

1. Work in a quiet room.

2. Work early in the day.

3. Review the Game Plan for your target score (see Lesson #1: It's About Time)

4. Don't use scrap paper. Get in the habit of writing on the test

5. Use a timer and WORK FOR THE FULL TIME. This is the one rule that kids break all the time. When you are doing a practice test, you will be eager to get it done with as soon as you can. But as you will see, learning to manage your test time is a big part of improving, so it's critical that you practice the right way.

6. Take this seriously! Fight for every point you can! Pretend it's REAL!

Follow these directions EVERY time you take a practice test. If you can't do it right, wait until you have a better time to do the test. There are only a limited number of actual tests that have been released so you don't want to waste one by giving a half-hearted effort.

But there is a much more important reason for taking practice tests seriously: you will score higher. And that will make you happier. Even though it is just practice, when your score goes up, you will be excited to see the improvement and motivated to keep working (like losing weight on a diet). But if you don't take the practice test seriously and your score doesn't go up, you will have trouble maintaining your effort. After all, as we know, it's ok to hate the SAT, and to resent having to spend time working on your score. So here is a riddle. Maybe it will cheer you up.

Q: What's worse than spending time to improve your SAT score?

A: Spending the time and NOT improving your score.

But that doesn't have to happen. You CAN improve your score. The strategies that I'm going to teach you are not complicated. You will read them and think that they are obvious, common-sense ideas that any one could use, if only some one would explain them. And that's exactly why I've written this book.

"Hey Mr. Keller, you want to hear something funny? I took [a nationally known SAT course] before I took your course. My score didn't change at all. Then I took your class and went up 120 points. I think that's funny."

- Student in line behind me at the cafeteria

Memo: About Calculators

Which one should you use? There are several ways to go here…

BASIC: You could just use a scientific calculator. Make sure that you know how to do fractions, decimals, exponents and roots.

ADVANCED: Use a graphing calculator. There may be one or two questions where it would be helpful to graph a line or graph a parabola. It is NOT essential, but having a graphing calculator would give you a slight edge.

MONSTER: Use a TI-89. This calculator is the most advanced one that is allowed on the SAT (and it definitely is allowed). But it is also intimidating to learn. Students have told me that they can't even figure out what to do after you turn it on. (You press the "Home" button.) And they complain that you tell it to divide and it doesn't. (Press the green diamond and then "Enter".) So why use it? I'll give you one really good reason: IT DOES ALGEBRA!

In other words, suppose you have an equation to solve. Let's say: $\dfrac{(3x-7)}{x} = 7$

Instead of solving this by hand, you could type F2 and then "Enter". This would open the equation solving function. Then, you type the equation followed by ",x)". So your screen looks like this:

Solve((3x-7)/x=7,x)

And then you hit "Enter" and watch the calculator spit out the right answer: **x = -7/4** !

For me, that one feature makes it worth having this calculator. But many of my students worry about giving up their familiar calculator. The good news is that you don't have to! You can bring TWO calculators to the SAT: the one you are used to and the TI89. If the TI89 helps you to solve just one or two questions, that's 20 more points added to your math score.

Still, since many students choose to go with the simpler calculator, for most of this book I am only going to assume that you have a basic scientific calculator. But I will occasionally offer alternatives only available on a graphing calculator or TI89.

PART I: "I say, you're going about it all wrong"
- *Famous Cartoon Chicken, Foghorn Leghorn*

How the SAT is biased against "Good" Students
How eleven years of traditional math instruction have hurt your SAT score
How to unlearn what school has taught you about doing math and taking tests

The first thing I want you to remember is that this is not school. Although you take the SAT when you are in high school, it is NOT a high school test. It contains only a little bit of high school math, much of which can be avoided. It isn't structured like a school test. It isn't graded like a school test. So say it with me: "THIS IS NOT SCHOOL!" You do NOT have to do things the way you were taught. You don't get partial credit for doing things by the book. All that matters is whether or not you grid in the right answer.

Then, you also need to understand that the SAT is biased, but not the way that you might think: **The SAT is biased against the "good student" who does things in the way they are taught in school.** So who does this bias favor? You may not like this but here goes: it's the kid who looks to cut corners. He's maybe even a little bit lazy. But in a resourceful kind of way. He doesn't always do what he's told, and because of this he is penalized in school with grades that are lower than the "good student". But on the SAT, this student is rewarded. Let's call him the non-conformist. **The SAT is biased in favor of the non-conformist.** Is it you? If it is, then you have no doubt experienced some school-related grief because of your failure to conform. But the SAT is going to give you a break, <u>once you learn how to take advantage of it!</u> And what if it isn't you? Then you need to understand the situation and change your approach (just on the SAT!) so that you benefit from this bias instead of being hurt by it.

Do you need convincing? Take a look at this problem:

$$\text{Given: } 5x + 2y = 8$$
$$3x - y = 5$$

$$\text{Find: } 2x + 3y$$

It certainly looks like a typical high school algebra problem, and you might think that that's why it is on the SAT. But you'd be wrong.

Use the rest of the space on this page to solve the problem BEFORE YOU LOOK AT MY SOLUTION. (I told you that you would have to work, too, remember? So do it.)

On the next page, I'm going to solve this problem for you, twice. First I'll do it the way you are taught in school. Then I'll do it the nonconformist's way. You decide which one you like better.

Given: $5x + 2y = 8$
$3x - y = 5$

Find: $2x + 3y$

Solution Method #1…the school way:

This is a pair of 2 equations and 2 unknowns.
I will use the method of simultaneous equations.

First I double the second equation.
That makes the number in front of the y's the same.

Then I add the equations.

Then solve for x.

Then plug x back into one of the two equations.

Then solve for y.

Now plug x and y into the expression we were asked to solve.

$$5x + 2y = 8$$
$$6x - 2y = 10$$
$$11x = 18$$
$$x = \frac{18}{11}$$

$$3 \times \frac{18}{11} - y = 5$$
$$\frac{54}{11} - y = \frac{55}{11}$$
$$y = -\frac{1}{11}$$

$$2 \times \frac{18}{11} + 3 \times (-\frac{1}{11}) =$$
$$\frac{36}{11} - \frac{3}{11} = \frac{33}{11} = 3$$

Hello? Hello? Are you still there? Did you fall asleep in the middle of that? Or even worse, are you now completely freaked out with anxiety because there's no way that you could do that problem in less than 20 minutes, if at all? Relax. Take deep cleansing breaths. Now look at method #2.

Given: $5x + 2y = 8$
$3x - y = 5$

Find: $2x + 3y$

Solution Method #2…the non-conformist way:

Hmm. There <u>must</u> be a way to get from the given information to the answer.

Let's see what happens if I add the equations…

$$5x + 2y = 8$$
$$\underline{3x - y = 5}$$
$$8x + y = 13$$

No, that's not it.

Ok, what if I subtract the equations?

$$5x + 2y = 8$$
$$\underline{3x - y = 5}$$
$$2x + 3y = 3$$

Hey look! That's it! I'm done.

OK, let's look at what just happened there. The poor kid who uses high school algebra needs a whole page of ugly math to solve this question and probably two or three minutes. But the non-conformist who plays around, hoping for a shortcut, gets his wish. And takes less than a minute. And it's lucky for him, because he could not have solved it the hard way -- he wasn't paying attention in class that day. He didn't do well on his math quiz that week, but he got it right on the SAT.

Now, some of you are thinking: "Wait a minute. That's cheap. The non-conformist was just lucky that adding or subtracting the equations just happened to land you on what you need. They could have written the problem with different numbers so that you HAVE to do it the hard way."

To which I respond: yes they COULD have written it that way, but they DIDN'T. From their point of view, the goal of the question was to see if you could find the easy connection. But if you want to torment yourself and waste time doing it the long, formal, in-school way, they will let you. But the non-conformist will finish faster than you and move on to the next question. Do you see what I mean? This test is biased. It's not fair.

What it comes down to is this: if you have been a non-conforming student your whole life, if you sleep in class, if you've occasionally been known to copy some one else's homework, or to trust your creativity to get you through tests, well then the SAT is written for you (and I think you are going to LOVE this book).

On the other hand, what if you are a "good" student? You do all your work, you take notes, you pay attention in class, you're a solid student, but the SAT is not designed for you. In fact, you know some of those non-conformists with lower grades than you but higher SAT scores. And it's making you mad. Talk about unfair. Let me reassure you, though. You have been a good student, good at learning what you have been taught. Your hard work has usually been rewarded. So now, I'm going to teach you something new – how to be creative and sneaky and how to cut corners. You can learn this way too. You might enjoy it, and it will raise your score. And then, back in school, you can continue to be the responsible, hard-working student that you have been all along. Only now you will be a hard working kid who also knows a few tricks.

Let's check your understanding so far:

Q: Why don't we want to use school methods on the SAT?

A: Because the SAT is NOT SCHOOL.

Try to keep that in mind as you continue working through this book.

Please turn the page and begin Lesson #1.

"I had a 460 on the first practice test, two weeks ago. Now I'm up to a 560. How sweet is that?"

- Sarah G.

Lesson #1: It's About <u>Time</u> !

If I could only teach you one thing about taking the SAT, this is what it would be:

SLOW DOWN!!! Stop trying to finish the sections!

Unless you have already earned above a 700 in previous practice tests, finishing the section is a mistake. I usually spend the first 30 minutes of every SAT course I teach explaining why this is true. I know it is hard to believe, for two reasons.

Reason #1: ETS tells you not to spend too much time on any problem. It's written in many of their pamphlets and is even part of the instructions the proctors read to you on the day of the test. ("Skip it and move on. You can return to the problem later if time remains." – sound familiar?)

Reason # 2: It goes against all of your school experience. Think about it. In school, you ALWAYS try to finish tests. If the bell rings before you get to the last page, you've had a bad day ("Oh, man! That test was impossible. I couldn't even finish!"). After all, those problems on the last page are usually the hardest ones and they are usually worth the most points. So in school, you need to make certain that you spend some time on them and at least earn some partial credit.

But, as I may have mentioned, THIS IS NOT SCHOOL! The SAT has a different set of rules:

<u>The hard problems and the easy problems are worth the same number of points!!!</u>

That may seem unfair. (Everything about the SAT seems unfair.) But we can adjust your strategy to take this into account.

<u>There is no partial credit for wrong answers. In fact, there is a PENALTY.</u>

In school, wrong answers are usually scored the same as blanks. But on the SAT, there is a penalty for getting things wrong. So your courage is NOT rewarded. In school, the grading system most teachers use encourages you to at least TRY every problem. By giving partial credit, we teachers send the message that ANYTHING is better than nothing. The SAT does just the opposite, so your strategy has to take this into account also.

<u>You can leave out a LOT of questions and still get a really good score.</u>

To give you a rough idea…

… You can omit 20%, get another 10% wrong and still be in the 600 neighborhood.
… You can omit 30%, get another 20% wrong and still be in the 500 neighborhood.

But why would you omit so many questions? Because they are HARD! And because you will lose points if you get them wrong. Your strategy has to take this into account, too.

So you see, the SAT is a different game, played by a different set of rules. And the first rule is to GO SLOW! There are problems on every SAT that you've been getting wrong simply because you were rushing. You rush because the little voice in your head says, "Move along, keep going or you'll never finish." But why would you want to finish? When you slow down, you will start getting those problems right, unlike those hard problems at the end, which you weren't getting right anyway. So why rush?

Still not convinced? Well, consider the following analogy…

The Basketball Shooting Contest

Suppose you are going to be in a basketball-shooting contest, not for something trivial like college admission, but for something you really care about: money!

The rules of the contest are:

1. You have 1 minute to shoot up to 25 times.

2. You may shoot only once from each of the numbered spots whether you make the shot or not.

3. You get $100 for every basket you make.

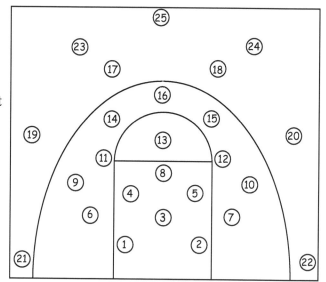

OK. You want to win the most money that you can. What's your strategy?

"Uh, I think I'll shoot as well and as fast as I can and hope to make a lot shots."

Well that's a good idea. In what order will you shoot them?

"I don't know. I might want to get the hard shots out of the way first."

Now that's NOT a good idea. You'd feel silly if time ran out before you shot the easiest ones.

"Oh, yeah. OK, easy shots first, hard ones later. Good thinking, coach."

Why are you shooting quickly?

"To shoot all 25 possible shots. Can't make 'em if you don't shoot 'em. Duh"

OK, good point. But wait a minute. Here comes a twist…

The Crucial Twist

Now, let's add a crucial twist: Suppose we change the rules so that while you still get $100 for every basket you make, you now LOSE $25 every time you miss. Does that change anything?

Think for a moment. Do you still want to shoot <u>all</u> the shots? Are you still going to hurry? NO and NO! What should you do instead? Now, your best bet is to shoot the shots that you have a pretty good chance of making, and that's all. You should NOT shoot any shot that is beyond your range. It wastes your time and costs you money. You are better off taking more time with the shots that you do have a good chance to make.

That's the general idea, but what if you need me to be more specific? What if you are thinking, "Tell me exactly which shots to attempt and which to skip."? I can't -- there is no single strategy that would work for everybody. Each player has to develop his or her own ideal game plan. To maximize your potential score now requires PLANNING.

First, you have to practice shooting. It will make you a better shooter, but it will also help you to learn what shots you are good at and what shots you are not.

Then, you have to decide in advance what shots you are going to take. In other words, what shots are worth risking $25 to attempt?

Finally, on the day of the contest, you attempt only those shots, and you take your time. You do NOT care that time will run out before you shoot the hard shots. Why not? Because:

1. By shooting slowly, you are making a higher percentage of the shots that are in your range.
2. The shots you didn't attempt are shots you probably would have lost money on anyway.

Even if time were not a factor, only the best shooters should attempt those last few shots. Most people would just be throwing money away. *"But sometimes I make that shot! I really think I can do it."* Yes, sometimes you do make that hard shot. But is it a good risk? It costs you money and time. You need to make a game plan, and follow it if you want to win at this game.

"But in basketball, I know how hard every shot is before I shoot it. On the SAT, how am I supposed to know how difficult the question is if I don't try to answer it?"

That is a really important question. The answer is…(drum roll, please)**… the questions are arranged in order of difficulty**. In every section, and every subsection, the early questions are easy, the later questions are harder and the last questions are just plain nasty. Knowing this, you can plan your strategy in advance, just like the basket shooter.

HOW TO MAP OUT YOUR GAME PLAN

Step 1: Set your score goal
Step 2: Plan which questions to answer and which to IGNORE

Determining Your Goal

Your strategy is based on the score you are aiming for. You should aim to improve your math score by around **100 points** from your most recent SAT or PSAT. Students who start with a lower score can expect bigger improvements. They have more room to improve and it's easier when you start lower. On the other hand, students who are already scoring high (let's say in the 600's) will find it harder to go up by as many points. Yes, the curve gets steeper at the top, but also, these students have less room to improve. Still, these techniques can raise their scores. One of my favorite students came to my SAT course with a 740 in math. He was really taking the course for the verbal help. But he paid attention to all of the math tricks and was happy to report to me that they helped him to an 800. He's at MIT now.

If you have never taken the SAT or PSAT, start by aiming for a 550 or 600. But then, you MUST do a practice test to see if you are in the right range.

Your "Raw Score" and the penalty for wrong answers

Your raw score is the number of questions you answer correctly, minus the penalties for all the ones you got wrong. Here's how it works: on every question, one of three things happens…

1. If you get it RIGHT, you earn 1 raw point.
2. If you leave it BLANK, you don't earn any raw points, but you don't lose any either.
3. If you get it WRONG, you lose either a quarter of a point on a multiple choice question. You don't lose any points for wrong grid-ins (but as you will see later, that does NOT mean you should answer them all). Another way to think of it is that in the 5-choice section, every four wrong answers cancel one of your right answers.

There is also a hidden penalty. Can you guess what it is? In addition to costing you points, getting things wrong is a WASTE OF TIME! (Think back to the basketball analogy.) That's why you want to learn and follow your game plan.

What's in a Game Plan?

The Game Plans show you what to answer and what to omit in each of the sections and subsections of the math SAT. There are three types of sections that you can tell apart instantly by the number of questions in each:

20-Questions: you get 25 minutes to answer 20 multiple questions of steadily increasing difficulty.

18-Questions: you get 25 minutes to answer 8 multiple choice questions followed by 10 "grid-in" questions. And each set follows the easy-medium-hard progression. This mea

16-Questions: you get 20 minutes to answer 16 multiple choice, again getting harder as you go.

More Bad News: The Experimental Sections

In case you are not already ticked off about having to take the SAT, here's something really irritating that you may have not heard about: the "experimental" sections. Of the more than three hours you spend testing, twenty-five minutes are spent taking a section that won't count toward your score. You might get an extra 25-minute math section on your SAT. And if you don't, you will get an extra 25-minute verbal section instead.[*]

The extra section does not count toward your score.
There is no way to tell which section is the "extra" one.
You have to do ALL of the sections as best you can.
ETS is using 25 minutes of your time to gather information for future tests.

THERE IS NOTHING YOU CAN DO ABOUT THIS!!!

Yes, I know, it's not fair...unfairness is everywhere. If it makes you feel better to know it, they use the information from the experimental section to figure out whether a problem is hard or easy. And then they put them in order for you. So this is an injustice that you benefit from in a small way. (But it still stinks.)

IMPORTANT NOTE:

The score goal you have selected today is only your FIRST STEP!!!

I expect my students to reach their first goal in a matter of weeks. And when you do, when you earn that score on a timed practice test, you should then look up the Game Plan for scoring 50 points higher, and start working toward that score. My most successful students have improved their math scores by 200 points when they were through. It could happen to you.

The Game Plans begin on the next page. Find the one that matches your goal and study it, but don't worry about memorizing it. You can even leave it open in front of you when you are taking your practice tests. By the time you have done a few practice tests, you will know your plan by heart. You can even bring your plan with you on the morning of the SAT and review it right up to the last minute. (Of course, you have to put it away when the test starts.)

The game plans on the next pages are also available on our website: www.satgameplan.com – you go to the website and then choose the "Interactive Math Strategy Guide". Then, click on the score you are aiming for and follow the instructions on the chart.

---

[*] That's why when you look at the exams in "The Official SAT Study Guide", the sections are numbered 1 – 10, but one of the numbered sections is missing. The missing section was the experimental section, which they do not include when they release the test to the public.

PRACTICE TEST ALERT: Once you have learned your Game Plan, it would be a good time to take a TIMED practice test (from *The Official SAT Study Guide*) to see how much easier it is when you use time properly.

Keller's Math SAT Game Plan   Target Score: <u>500</u>

Work your way SLOWLY through your "Answer Zone". Be PATIENT with yourself and give yourself time to READ, THINK and PLAY. Don't skip easier questions just to end up wasting time on harder ones!

Section-by-section Breakdown:

20 Question Section

Answer Zone												Skip Zone							
1	2	3	4	5	6	7	8	9	10	11	12	13	14	15	16	17	18	19	20

18 Question Section

Answer Zone					Skip Zone			Answer Zone						Skip Zone			
1	2	3	4	5	6	7	8	9	10	11	12	13	14	15	16	17	18

16 Question Section

Answer Zone										Skip Zone					
1	2	3	4	5	6	7	8	9	10	11	12	13	14	15	16

What is the best score I can get with this strategy?

If you answer all of the "Answer Zone" correctly, you will score around a 550. You can miss 6 or 7 and still get a 500!

Should I EVER attempt a question in the "Skip Zone?

Yes, but only if you happen to recognize a specific problem type where you have learned the trick. For example, the "Back Door play" (see Lesson #3) shows up often in the "Skip Zone", so that gives you a chance to steal some points.

Can I EVER skip a question inside the "Answer Zone"?

Hmmm. Well. Yes, but only if it's late in the zone and it's on a topic that you are especially weak in. For example, some students will skip late geometry questions. But the basic rule is: once you spend time on it, ANSWER IT!

What if a "Skip Zone" question looks easy?

Unless it matches a method you have learned in this book, I'd be VERY careful. The SAT is very good at making things look easier than they are. It's in the "Skip Zone" for a reason.

What is an "Answer Zone" question seems to hard?

You are probably over-thinking, or even more likely, misreading the question. Go back and take another look, SLOWLY! It's going to be easier than it looks. It's in the "Answer Zone" for a reason.

ALSO STUDY THE REMINDERS ON THE OTHER SIDE OF THIS SHEET!!!

Things to remember as you are about to begin:

1. Go SLOOOOWWWW. As slow as you can make yourself go. The questions you are rushing through are easier than the ones that you are rushing to.

2. PLAY!!! Draw pictures. Make lists. Take guesses. It's NOT school.

3. Avoid algebra! Go to their answers and ask, "Could THIS be it? Let's see…"

4. Avoid algebra! Use the Back Door play[*]. Make up your own numbers that fit.

5. It's going fine. It isn't any harder than the practice tests you have done. It just seems harder now that it counts. Take a deep breath, calm down, and keep playing.

6. USE YOUR CALCULATOR (Especially, TI89! F2, Enter…)

7. READ EVERY WORD! The words you skip are the reasons you get an easy question wrong.

8. Be slow and bold! Once you spend time on a question, go ahead and answer it. But don't be in a hurry to answer more questions than you should. FOLLOW YOUR GAME PLAN!

9. Take your breaks! You are entitled to one break after every hour. Use it. Get up. Wake up. Have a drink. Eat a snack. Get ready to start a new section.

10. Relax, and play your game. Don't worry if you think you've gotten one wrong. You are going to make mistakes. That's OK. Just stay in your plan, and keep doing your best.

---

[*] Covered in Lesson #3

Keller's Math SAT Game Plan

Target Score: <u>550</u>

Work your way SLOWLY through your "Answer Zone". Be PATIENT with yourself and give yourself time to READ, THINK and PLAY. Don't skip easier questions just to end up wasting time on harder ones!

Section-by-section Breakdown:

20 Question Section

Answer Zone														Skip Zone					
1	2	3	4	5	6	7	8	9	10	11	12	13	14	15	16	17	18	19	20

18 Question Section

Answer Zone						Skip		Answer Zone						Skip Zone			
1	2	3	4	5	6	7	8	9	10	11	12	13	14	15	16	17	18

16 Question Section

Answer Zone											Skip Zone				
1	2	3	4	5	6	7	8	9	10	11	12	13	14	15	16

What is the best score I can get with this strategy?

If you answer all of the "Answer Zone" correctly, you will score around a 590. You can miss 4 or 5 and still get a 550!

Should I EVER attempt a question in the "Skip Zone?

Yes, but only if you happen to recognize a specific problem type where you have learned the trick. For example, the "Back Door play" (see Lesson #3) shows up often in the "Skip Zone", so that gives you a chance to steal some points.

Can I EVER skip a question inside the "Answer Zone"?

Hmmm. Well. Yes, but only if it's late in the zone and it's on a topic that you are especially weak in. For example, some students will skip late geometry questions. But the basic rule is: once you spend time on it, ANSWER IT!

What if a "Skip Zone" question looks easy?

Unless it matches a method you have learned in this book, I'd be VERY careful. The SAT is very good at making things look easier than they are. It's in the "Skip Zone" for a reason.

What is an "Answer Zone" question seems to hard?

You are probably over-thinking, or even more likely, misreading the question. Go back and take another look, SLOWLY! It's going to be easier than it looks. It's in the "Answer Zone" for a reason.

ALSO STUDY THE REMINDERS ON THE OTHER SIDE OF THIS SHEET!!!

Things to remember as you are about to begin:

1. Go SLOOOOWWWW. As slow as you can make yourself go. The questions you are rushing through are easier than the ones that you are rushing to.

2. PLAY!!! Draw pictures. Make lists. Take guesses. It's NOT school.

3. Avoid algebra! Go to their answers and ask, "Could THIS be it? Let's see…"

4. Avoid algebra! Use the Back Door play*. Make up your own numbers that fit.

5. It's going fine. It isn't any harder than the practice tests you have done. It just seems harder now that it counts. Take a deep breath, calm down, and keep playing.

6. USE YOUR CALCULATOR (Especially, TI89! F2, Enter…)

7. READ EVERY WORD! The words you skip are the reasons you get an easy question wrong.

8. Be slow and bold! Once you spend time on a question, go ahead and answer it. But don't be in a hurry to answer more questions than you should. FOLLOW YOUR GAME PLAN!

9. Take your breaks! You are entitled to one break after every hour. Use it. Get up. Wake up. Have a drink. Eat a snack. Get ready to start a new section.

10. Relax, and play your game. Don't worry if you think you've gotten one wrong. You are going to make mistakes. That's OK. Just stay in your plan, and keep doing your best.

---

* Covered in Lesson #3

Keller's Game Plan

Target Score: 600

Work your way SLOWLY through your "Answer Zone". Be PATIENT with yourself and give yourself time to READ, THINK and PLAY. Don't skip easier questions just to end up wasting time on harder ones!

Section-by-section Breakdown:

20 Question Section

																Skip Zone			
						Answer Zone													
1	2	3	4	5	6	7	8	9	10	11	12	13	14	15	16	17	18	19	20

18 Question Section

					Skip								Skip Zone		
	Answer Zone							Answer Zone							
1	2	3	4	5	6	7	8	9	10	11	12	13	14	15	16	17	18

16 Question Section

												Skip Zone		
					Answer Zone									
1	2	3	4	5	6	7	8	9	10	11	12	13	14	15	16

What is the best score I can get with this strategy?

If you answer all of the "Answer Zone" correctly, you will score around a 640. You can miss 3 or 4 and still get a 600!

Should I EVER attempt a question in the "Skip Zone?

Yes, but only if you happen to recognize a specific problem type where you have learned the trick. For example, the "Back Door play" (see Lesson #3) shows up often in the "Skip Zone", so that gives you a chance to steal some points.

Can I EVER skip a question inside the "Answer Zone"?

Hmmm. Well. Yes, but only if it's late in the zone and it's on a topic that you are especially weak in. For example, some students will skip late geometry questions. But the basic rule is: once you spend time on it, ANSWER IT!

What if a "Skip Zone" question looks easy?

Unless it matches a method you have learned in this book, I'd be VERY careful. The SAT is very good at making things look easier than they are. It's in the "Skip Zone" for a reason.

What is an "Answer Zone" question seems to hard?

You are probably over-thinking, or even more likely, misreading the question. Go back and take another look, SLOWLY! It's going to be easier than it looks. It's in the "Answer Zone" for a reason.

ALSO STUDY THE REMINDERS ON THE OTHER SIDE OF THIS SHEET!!!

Things to remember as you are about to begin:

1. Go SLOOOOWWWW. As slow as you can make yourself go. The questions you are rushing through are easier than the ones that you are rushing to.

2. PLAY!!! Draw pictures. Make lists. Take guesses. It's NOT school.

3. Avoid algebra! Go to their answers and ask, "Could THIS be it? Let's see…"

4. Avoid algebra! Use the Back Door play[*]. Make up your own numbers that fit.

5. It's going fine. It isn't any harder than the practice tests you have done. It just seems harder now that it counts. Take a deep breath, calm down, and keep playing.

6. USE YOUR CALCULATOR (Especially, TI89! F2, Enter…)

7. READ EVERY WORD! The words you skip are the reasons you get an easy question wrong.

8. Be slow and bold! Once you spend time on a question, go ahead and answer it. But don't be in a hurry to answer more questions than you should. FOLLOW YOUR GAME PLAN!

9. Take your breaks! You are entitled to one break after every hour. Use it. Get up. Wake up. Have a drink. Eat a snack. Get ready to start a new section.

10. Relax, and play your game. Don't worry if you think you've gotten one wrong. You are going to make mistakes. That's OK. Just stay in your plan, and keep doing your best.

---

[*] Covered in Lesson #3

Keller's Game Plan   Target Score: __650__

PLEASE NOTE: A HIGHER SCORE GOAL REQUIRES YOUR GAME PLAN TO BE MORE SUBTLE...

There are no questions that are automatically too hard for you to try. However, you need to use time wisely. Start by moving SLOWLY through the "Answer Zone". Your goal is to sweep those questions. Then, only if you still have time, pick and choose one or two questions from the "Scan Zone." In the end, you should attempt not quite half of the "Scan Zone". But how do you choose? Look for:

1. Problems that you can do by trial and error
2. Problems that you can do by the Back Door Trick
3. Problems that don't look like high school math—the stranger the better!

In general, you'll find that you can trust your own judgment. And that means if you don't like ANY of the "Scan Zone" questions in a given section, feel free to skip them all. Your first job is to sweep the "Answer Zone".

Section-by-section Breakdown:

20 Question Section

								Answer Zone								Scan Zone		
1	2	3	4	5	6	7	8	9	10	11	12	13	14	15	16	17	18	19	20

18 Question Section

		Answer Zone				Scan			Answer Zone					Scan Zone		
1	2	3	4	5	6	7	8	9	10	11	12	13	14	15	16	17	18

16 Question Section

				Answer Zone									Scan Zone		
1	2	3	4	5	6	7	8	9	10	11	12	13	14	15	16

AND STUDY THE REMINDERS ON THE OTHER SIDE OF THIS SHEET!!!

Things to remember as you are about to begin:

1. Go SLOOOOWWWW. As slow as you can make yourself go. The questions you are rushing through are easier than the ones that you are rushing to.

2. PLAY!!! Draw pictures. Make lists. Take guesses. It's NOT school.

3. Avoid algebra! Go to their answers and ask, "Could THIS be it? Let's see..."

4. Avoid algebra! Use the Back Door play[*]. Make up your own numbers that fit.

5. It's going fine. It isn't any harder than the practice tests you have done. It just seems harder now that it counts. Take a deep breath, calm down, and keep playing.

6. USE YOUR CALCULATOR (Especially, TI89! F2, Enter...)

7. READ EVERY WORD! The words you skip are the reasons you get an easy question wrong.

8. Be slow and bold! Once you spend time on a question, go ahead and answer it. But don't be in a hurry to answer more questions than you should. FOLLOW YOUR GAME PLAN!

9. Take your breaks! You are entitled to one break after every hour. Use it. Get up. Wake up. Have a drink. Eat a snack. Get ready to start a new section.

10. Relax, and play your game. Don't worry if you think you've gotten one wrong. You are going to make mistakes. That's OK. Just stay in your plan, and keep doing your best.

---

[*] Covered in Lesson #3

Keller's Game Plan

Target Score: 700 +

Plan on attempting <u>nearly</u> all of the questions. Plan on ignoring the two or three hardest questions.

PLEASE NOTE: A HIGHER SCORE GOAL REQUIRES YOUR GAME PLAN TO BE MORE SUBTLE...

There are no questions that are automatically too hard for you to try. However, you need to use time wisely. Start by moving SLOWLY through the "Answer Zone". Your goal is to sweep those questions. Then, only if you still have time, pick and choose one or two questions from the "Scan Zone." In the end, you should attempt two thirds of the "Scan Zone". But how do you choose? Look for:

　　　　1. Problems that you can do by trial and error
　　　　2. Problems that you can do by the Back Door Trick
　　　　3. Problems that don't look like high school math—the stranger the better!

In general, you'll find that you can trust your own judgment. And that means if you don't like ANY of the "Scan Zone" questions in a given section, feel free to skip them all. Your first job is to sweep the "Answer Zone".

Section-by-section Breakdown:

20 Question Section

																Scan Zone			
Answer Zone																			
1	2	3	4	5	6	7	8	9	10	11	12	13	14	15	16	17	18	19	20

18 Question Section

Answer Zone						Scan		Answer Zone							Scan Zone		
1	2	3	4	5	6	7	8	9	10	11	12	13	14	15	16	17	18

16 Question Section

Answer Zone													Scan Zone		
1	2	3	4	5	6	7	8	9	10	11	12	13	14	15	16

AND STUDY THE REMINDERS ON THE OTHER SIDE OF THIS SHEET!!!

Things to remember as you are about to begin:

1. Go SLOOOOWWWW. As slow as you can make yourself go. The questions you are rushing through are easier than the ones that you are rushing to.

2. PLAY!!! Draw pictures. Make lists. Take guesses. It's NOT school.

3. Avoid algebra! Go to their answers and ask, "Could THIS be it? Let's see…"

4. Avoid algebra! Use the Back Door play[*]. Make up your own numbers that fit.

5. It's going fine. It isn't any harder than the practice tests you have done. It just seems harder now that it counts. Take a deep breath, calm down, and keep playing.

6. USE YOUR CALCULATOR (Especially, TI89! F2, Enter…)

7. READ EVERY WORD! The words you skip are the reasons you get an easy question wrong.

8. Be slow and bold! Once you spend time on a question, go ahead and answer it. But don't be in a hurry to answer more questions than you should. FOLLOW YOUR GAME PLAN!

9. Take your breaks! You are entitled to one break after every hour. Use it. Get up. Wake up. Have a drink. Eat a snack. Get ready to start a new section.

10. Relax, and play your game. Don't worry if you think you've gotten one wrong. You are going to make mistakes. That's OK. Just stay in your plan, and keep doing your best.

---

[*] Covered in Lesson #3

Lesson #2: No Algebra, Please.

We LOVE trial and error. And it's OK to be wrong.

There is something strange about how we teach math in high school. There is very little time for playful exploration, for making guesses, for daring to be wrong. Most students experience math class as a place where you are taught the proper methods for solving a specific set of problem types: <u>This</u> is how you complete the square. <u>This</u> is how you rationalize a denominator. <u>This</u> is how you graph a cosine function. Follow the procedure. Do it my way. Guessing has no place here. The only people who guess are the truly desperate.

Now maybe this is just the way it has to be (though I doubt it). But guessing is a legitimate mathematical technique. Professional mathematicians use it all the time, especially when they are just beginning to work on a problem. Now, you may not go on to become a professional mathematician, but you *are* going to take the SAT. Learning to guess and learning to play with a problem will give you an advantage.

So, here is the SECOND piece of advice I give to students (this is Lesson #2, for those of you who are keeping score at home).

Don't feel guilty about guessing. Don't feel guilty about using trial and error.

Whenever you are stuck, especially if you are lost in some algebraic mess, use trial and error. One at a time, with either their answer choices or your own guesses, keep asking yourself:

"Could THIS be the answer? What if it were? Let's see if it works…"

Then, play with it and see if it fits the question. If it does, great – you've got the answer. If not, try another guess.

I'm going to show you a bunch of examples of SAT-type problems that COULD be solved algebraically. But the solutions I will demonstrate do not use algebra. If that makes you happier, skip the next paragraph and go to the first sample. But if the thought of avoiding all that algebra makes you uncomfortable, because you PREFER doing algebra, the next paragraph is for you.

"But I <u>like</u> doing algebra…"

Don't feel embarrassed. Actually, you are not alone. Many students tell me that they are more comfortable using algebra to solve problems. And that's OK. But on the SAT, there are times when you will not be able to come up with the right equations to solve. Or you just might not be able to solve them. Please be open-minded and try my way. Then, at least you will have a new alternative. Besides, I predict that once you get the hang of it, you'll see that trial and error is an amazingly useful trick.

Example #1: First try this by using algebra— **If $(2x - 2)^2 = 64$, and $x > 0$, find x.**

How did you do? Well, let's look at the answer choices:

a) 4   b) 5   c) 6   d) 7   e) 8

I am NOT going to show you the algebraic solution. Instead, I am going to ask you a question:

Could the answer to this question be 'a'? In other words, does x = 4?

You might think that you can't answer that question if you have not found the solution yet. But you CAN! Just take x=4 and plug it into the equation and see if it works!

$(2x - 2)^2 = 64$

Is $x = 4$?

Let's see…2 times 4 is 8. 8 – 2 = 6. $6^2 = 36$, which is NOT 64. So 'a' is NOT the answer.

Now what? Oh, yeah…let's try the next answer choice.

Is $x = 5$?

Let's see…2 times 5 is 10, 10 – 2 = 8, $8^2 = 64$…It works! I'm done!

So what have we learned here? It's that, when it comes to finding answers to algebraic equations,

Checking solutions is easier than *finding* solutions!!!

You would think that ETS would stop putting this kind of question on the test. If there is just a single equation for you to solve, the trial-and-error method makes it simple. In fact, there are certain graphing calculators (such as the TI-89) that can solve these equations for you. Still, ETS continues to use this problem type. But they do try to make it a little harder…Here's one with two equations and two unknowns:

$$2x + y = 12$$
$$x^2 + 2y^2 = 33$$

Find a possible value for x.

The school method involves solving the first equation for y, substituting the expression into the second equation, "foil"-ing, distributing, regrouping, factoring and then solving. Try it here…

Now tell the truth: did you really try the school method? Or did you just skip it? If you skipped it, then….GOOD JOB! I'm proud of you. It means that you are getting the idea that the school way wastes time. Let's try it another way…

$$2x + y = 12$$
$$x^2 + 2y^2 = 33$$

What if we look at the answer choices and play "Could THIS be it?"

a) 3   b) 4   c) 5   d) 6   e) 7

Is $x=3$? Let's see….$2\cdot3 + y = 12$, $6 + y = 12$ so $y = 6$.
But then $3^2 + 2\cdot6^2 = 81$, which is NOT 33. So x isn't 3.

Is $x=4$? Let's see….$2\cdot4 + y = 12$, $8 + y = 12$ so $y = 4$.
But then $4^2 + 2\cdot4^2 = 48$, which is NOT 33. So x isn't 4.

Is $x=5$? Let's see….$2\cdot5 + y = 12$, $10 + y = 12$ so $y = 2$.
But then $5^2 + 2\cdot2^2 = 33$, which is CORRECT!!!

Now, students sometimes object to this procedure, claiming that it takes too long. To which I have three responses:

1. What's your hurry? You are supposed to be taking your time!

2. After you practice the trial and error method for a while, you get quicker at it.

3. Did you get this right using school math? Or did you even try? By traditional methods, this is a pretty tough problem. ***Using a method that takes time but actually gets you the answer is better than not getting the answer at all, fast or slow!***

TRIAL AND ERROR WITH WORD PROBLEMS

The last examples showed what to do when the problem gives you equations that you have to solve. But they don't always give you the equations. Sometimes, they expect you to figure out the equation for yourself. I'm talking about word problems. Many of you dislike word problems so much that you skip them almost automatically. But you don't have to skip them, and you don't have to do algebra. Trial and error works here as well.

Let's see how this works…

The sum of four consecutive integers is 82. Find the greatest of the four integers.

If you have not been convinced yet, feel free to do this problem by algebra.
The non-conformist method is shown below. (And the non-conformist himself has already skipped to the solutions!)

The sum of four consecutive integers is 82. Find the greatest of the four integers.

a) 19   b) 20   c) 21   d) 22   e) 23   [I'm going straight to the easy way.]

Is it 'a'? In other words, is 19 the greatest of the four consecutive integers?
Then, the integers would have to be 16, 17, 18, 19. Let's see if it works.
16+17+18+19=70, which is NOT 82. It's too small. I think I'll try 'e' next.

Is it 'e'? In other words, is 23 the greatest of the four consecutive integers?
Then, the integers would have to be 20, 21, 22, 23. Let's see if it works.
20+21+22+23=86, which is NOT 82. It's a little too big. I think I'll try 'd' next.

Is it 'd'? In other words, is 22 the greatest of the four consecutive integers?
Then, the integers would have to be 19, 20, 21, 22. Let's see if it works.
19+20+21+22=82, which is CORRECT. And we're done. With no algebra!

In the examples that follow, I have chosen to make 'B' the correct answer. This is because, for the purpose of teaching you this method, it is important that you see at least one wrong answer before seeing the answer that turns out to be right. On the actual SAT, there is no pattern. Sometimes, the first answer you try works and sometimes you have to try them all. There is no pattern. None. In fact, paying attention to the pattern of your answers is one of those *"50 Habits of Insane People"*. Please do not interpret my using 'B' so frequently as a recommendation to choose 'B' on the actual test. There is NO pattern. None. Now, more examples…

On a certain bridge, there is a toll of $3 for cars and $5 for trucks. From 50 vehicles, all either cars or trucks, a total of $210 in tolls was collected. How many of the vehicles were cars?

a) 15   b) 20   c)....whatever....

Is it 'a'? If there were 15 cars, then since 50 – 15 = 35, there were 35 trucks.
The 15 cars pay 15·3 = $45, the 35 trucks pay 35·5 = $175.
$45 + $175 = $220, which is not $210 so the answer is NOT 'a'.

Is it 'b'? If there were 20 cars, then since 50 – 20 = 30, there were 30 trucks.
The 20 cars pay 20·3 = $60, the 30 trucks pay 30·5 = $150.
$60 + $150 = $210, which is CORRECT! We are done. And no algebra, again!

*   *   *   *   *   *   *   *   *   *

Here's a really obnoxious one[*]...

Mary is 15 years older than Tom. Nine years from now, her age will be three less than twice what his age is then. How old is Tom now?

a) 3   b) 9   c)...whatever...

Is it 'a'? If Tom is 3, then Mary is 3+15=18.
So in 9 years, Tom will be 3+9=12 and Mary will be 18+9=27.
But 27 is NOT 3 less than twice 12. So the answer is not 'a'.

Is it 'b'? If Tom is 9, then Mary is 9+15=24.
So in 9 years, Tom will be 9+9=18 and Mary will be 24+9=33.
And 33 IS 3 less than twice 18. So 'b" is CORRECT! We are done. And no algebra, again!

*   *   *   *   *   *   *   *   *

Most SAT's include three or four problems that can be done by trial and error, which is reason enough to learn this method. But also, as you learn this method, you start to let go of your instinct to do things the way you do them in school. When that happens, your score rises, because (as I may have mentioned once or twice) THIS IS NOT SCHOOL.

---

[*] You probably hate this kind of problem. Here's why: it's STUPID and pointless. Algebra books usually include problems like these, ironically, to demonstrate how useful algebra really is. I think of this kind of problem as the mathematical equivalent of word-search puzzles – fun, if you like that sort of thing, but useless.

Here's a silly one:

At a family picnic, children and dogs are playing in the backyard. Aunt Lisa looks out in the yard and counts 18 heads and 50 legs. How many dogs are in the yard? (You may assume that the dogs have 4 legs each, and the kids have 2 legs each.)

a) 7   b) 8   c) 9   d) 10   e) 11

OK, this time, suppose we start with answer choice c:

Suppose there are 9 dogs. Then they have 9x4=36 legs. So we need 14 more legs to get to 50. That means 7 kids. But 9+7 does not add up to 18 heads. So it's not 'c'.

Now, we can save time if we notice that to get more heads, we need fewer dog legs. If you don't notice this, that's OK too. Just pick another answer and start playing. So let's try 'a':

Suppose there are 7 dogs. That would be 7x4=28 legs. Need 22 more to get to 50. That means 11 kids. And 11 + 7 = 18. Yes!

(You could also reason this out in the opposite order: start by making the heads come out right and then work on the legs. Either way works.)

Before you turn to the practice problems, let's look back at what have we learned:

1. Don't do algebra. Don't write equations. Don't solve equations.
2. Go to each answer choice and PLAY with it...see if it works.

This is assuming, of course, that there are answer choices to choose from. But what if you are working in the "Grid-in" section, where there are no answer choices? You can STILL use trial and error. I will show you how in Lesson #4. But for now, there are practice problems on the next page which can all be done by trial and error. In addition, when you move into Part II of this book, and you are working on those practice problems, be on the lookout for trial and error problems there as well.

Practice Set #1: Trial and Error

1. If three more than a number is the same as three times that number, then the number is:

a) 0   b) 1   c) 1.5   d) –3   e) –1/2

2. The first of four consecutive even integers is 32 less than the sum of the last three. What is the first of the four?

a) 10   b) 12   c) 14   d) 15   e) 16

3. A theater sells general admissions tickets and reserved seating tickets. A reserved seating ticket costs $4 more than a general admission ticket. When they sold 120 general admission seats and 80 reserved seats, they took in a total of $1920 in sales. How much did they charge for the general admissions ticket?

a) $5   b) $6   c) $7   d) $8   e) $9

4. Jack drives home from college every few weeks, usually averaging 50 miles per hour for the trip. Then, he discovered that if he increased his average speed to 60 miles per hour, he could shorten his trip by 30 minutes. How long is the trip?

a) 75 miles   b) 125 miles   c) 150 miles   d) 175 miles   e) 300 miles

5. When a number is divided by 6, the remainder is twice as big as the remainder you get when the same number is divided by 5. Which of the following could be the number?

a) 18   b) 22   c) 28   d) 45   e) 49

6. Marcia is three times as old as Barbara. But six years from now, she will only be twice as old as Barbara. How old is Barbara now?

a) 4   b) 6   c) 9   d) 12   e) 15

Set #1 Answer Key

For each one of these, the method is the same: pick an answer choice, see if it works. If not, pick another…
(For those of you who insist on using algebraic solutions, go ask your algebra teacher ☺)

1. We are going to add 3 to a number and see if we get the same result as when we triple the number instead, starting with answer 'a' and moving on…
0+3=3, 0x3=0…no
1+3=4, 1x3=3…no
1.5+3=4.5, 1.5 x 3 = 4.5…YES!
ANSWER: c

2. If 10 is the first of the four then the numbers are 10, 12, 14, and 16. The sum of the last three is 12+14+16 = 42. And, since 42 IS 32 more than the first number, answer 'a' is correct.
ANSWER: a

3. Could the answer be 'a'? If the general admission seats are $5, then the reserved seats are $4 dollars more which makes them $9. So the money they take in is $5 x 120 + $9 x 80 = $1320. But that's too low. So next I'll try 'c'.
If the general admission are $7 then the reserved are $11. $7 x 120 + $11 x 80 = $1720…still too low.
Now 'd': If the generals are $8 and the reserves are $12, then it's $8 x 120 + $12 x 80 = $1920. YES!
ANSWER: d

4. Let's try 'e' first: If the trip is 300 miles, then at 50 miles per hour it would take 300/50 = 6 hours. But at 60 miles per hour it would take 300/60 = 5 hours. That's a savings of a full hour or 60 minutes. So that's not the answer. In fact, it's twice as much savings as we are looking for! So a good next guess would be 'c'. (But if you don't realize this, it doesn't matter – you'll still get it eventually.) If the trip is 150 miles, then at 50 miles per hour, it would take 150/50=3 hours. And at 60 miles per hour, it would take 150/6 = 2.5 hours for a savings of a half hour, which is 30 minutes. **ANSWER: c**

5. First of all, if you are in need of a review of remainders, see page 69. Once you remember how to find remainders, this question is just a matter of checking each choice:
a) 18/6 = 3 r 0 and 18/5 = 3 r 3…but 0 is not twice as big as 3.
b) 22/6 = 3 r 4 and 22/5 = 4 r 2…4 IS twice as big as 2
ANSWER: b

6. Is Barbara 4? Then Marcia must be 12 (which is 3x as old). So 6 years from now, Barbara will be 10 and Marcia will be 18. But 18 is not twice as old as 10. So Barbara is not 4.
Is Barbara 6? Then Marcia would have to be 18 (which is 3x6). And 6 years from now, Barbara would be 12 and Marcia would be 24. And since 24 IS twice as old as 12, this must be the right answer.
ANSWER: b

On to Lesson #3!

Lesson #3: The Back Door Play

Transforming Algebra Problems into Arithmetic Problems

The trick I am about to teach you is my favorite SAT trick of all time. It's the trick that, more so than any other, makes you feel like you are getting away with something. I call it the Back Door, because at the key moment in the problem, instead of going through the front door with algebra, you get to go around to the back door with arithmetic. Also, this is the SAT trick that works on school tests as well. It is not so easy to write multiple-choice questions that actually force students to use algebra. ETS rarely succeeds. This is a trick worth knowing.

Note: it is going to take me a couple of pages to explain how to use the "Back Door". But once you get the hang of it, it's easy and quick. In fact, it feels like magic. Just stay with me here for a little while…

How to Recognize a "Back Door" Problem

1. Read the question carefully (as always). Do you see any algebraic variables? (Don't forget to look at the diagrams. The SAT likes to put algebra into their geometry questions. But the Back Door play takes the algebra out of them again.) If you see variables in the question, it might be a Back Door problem.

2. Next, look at the answer choices. Do at least some of them also have algebraic variables? Now, it is almost certain that the problem you are looking at is open to the Back Door play.

Here is a typical example:

In a high school club that has 50 students as members, 20 members are seniors, n members are juniors and $2n$ are sophomores, where n is an integer and $0 < n < 10$. If the remaining members are freshmen, then in terms of n, what percent of the members are freshmen?

> a) $7n$ %
> b) $(30 - 3n)\%$
> c) $(50 - 3n)\%$
> d) $(60 - 6n)\%$
> e) $(100 - 6n)\%$

Once you know what to look for, the characteristics that identify a Back Door Problem really jump off the page. It helps that the SAT always prints algebraic variables in italics. Also, this particular example has one other clue that screams, "I am a Back Door Problem!" It's the phrase "**…in terms of…**" which is the SAT's way of telling you that the answer you are looking for is an algebraic expression, and not a number. But wouldn't you rather work with numbers? That is precisely what the Back Door play is going to do for you – let you use numbers instead of algebraic expressions.

"But I like algebra!" (You, again?)

Even if you are very comfortable with algebra, learn the Back Door play thoroughly before you decide. I'm pretty good at algebra myself, but the Back Door play is so simple that I end up using it all the time.

The Back Door play in 3 Easy Steps:

1. Make up numbers for each of the variables

That's it? Just make them up? ANY numbers? Well, almost any numbers. There are a couple of rules to remember about the numbers you make up:

i. The numbers you make up should be easy but not the most obvious numbers. If it is possible, avoid using 0, 1 and 2. And if the problem is about angles, avoid 30, 45 and 60 degrees. But what if you forget to follow this rule, and your numbers are too obvious? Usually, the method works anyway, and if it doesn't work, it tells you so. Stay tuned…

ii. The numbers you make up must fit the problem. What that means is that if the problem describes the variables, you have to pick numbers that match the description. And if there is an equation that relates the variables, your numbers have to work when you plug them into the equation. Sometimes, this takes TIME. Do not rush. If your numbers don't fit the problem, you won't get anywhere. Also, the harder it is to find numbers that fit, the easier the rest of the problem will be. So take your time and get this step right.

iii. If you are making up numbers to fit an equation and you find yourself completely stuck, consider making up the numbers in a different order. Usually, one order is easier than another. Or try starting over with numbers that are easier to work with.

Let's take another look at the sample problem and make up a number…

In a high school club that has 50 students as members, 20 members are seniors, n members are juniors and $2n$ are sophomores, where n is an integer and $0 < n < 10$. If the remaining members are freshmen, then in terms of n, what percent of the members are freshmen?

Hmm…We need to make up a number for n. Must be an integer. Between 0 and 10.
OK, I'll try n = 5.

That's it. We are done with Step 1. And notice that you don't want to spend a lot of time tormenting yourself looking for the perfect number. Just make up a number that fits what they say and then get on with it. If you come to a point where you wish you had chosen different numbers, well then you can always change your numbers then. But for now, we've made up a number and it's on to step 2.

2. Use <u>your</u> numbers to work out the answer to <u>their</u> question.

Start by re-reading the question, now that you have replaced the variables with numbers. It will seem easier. And then, to solve the problem, you will be doing arithmetic instead of algebra. The answer you get will be a number, not an algebraic expression. It won't be "in terms of" any letters. And that is OK – it's just what is supposed to happen with this method.

Let's re-read the sample problem. Now, it's <u>as if</u> it said:

In a high school club that has 50 students as members, 20 members are seniors, 5 members are juniors and 10 are sophomores. If the remaining members are freshmen, what percent of the members are freshmen?

It looks so much simpler after you replace the n with a 5 and the 2n with a 10.
And, of course, we are going to ignore the whole "in terms of n" business, and do this as an arithmetic problem.

Let's see…50 students total…20 + 5 + 10 = 35 accounted for…50 –35 = 15 so 15 0f the 50 are freshman. And 15 out of 50 is 30%. So my answer is 30%.

 And that's it for step 2. Do not let it bother you that your answer (30%) does not look like any of the answer choices. Step 3 will take care of that for us.

3. Go around to the Back Door!

Look at the answer choices. The reason none of them match your answer yet is that your answer was based on the decision to let n = 5. So now, you have to substitute n = 5 into each of the answer choices. Then, any choice that doesn't match your answer is wrong!

Let's see what happens. Remember, our answer is 30 and our value for n is 5…

a) $7n$ %	*7x5=35…which is not 30*
b) $(30 – 3n)$%	*30 – 3x5 = 30 –15 = 15…which is not 30*
c) $(50 – 3n)$%	*50 – 3x5 = 50 – 15 = 35…which is not 30*
d) $(60 – 6n)$%	*60 – 6x5 = 60 – 30 = 30…AHA! We have a match!*
e) $(100 – 6n)$%	*100 – 6x5 = 100 – 30 = 70…which is not 30.*

And so the answer is D.

You might be wondering why you should continue to check ALL of the answers after you have already found the one that matches your answer. The answer is simple: sometimes, you get more than one match. It doesn't happen too often to people who avoid the obvious numbers, but it does happen occasionally, so you always need to check all the answers and you need to know what to do if you get more than one match.

When you get more than one matching answer:

Go back to step 1 (where you made up numbers to fit the question)... Make up DIFFERENT numbers.

Then, repeat step 2 (where you solved their question). You will now have a new answer to their question.

Then, repeat step 3 (where you substitute your numbers into their answers), but you do NOT have to check all of the answers, only the answers that worked with your original numbers. They won't all work again.

Let's try another:

If a square's area = x, which of the following expressions gives the perimeter, p in terms of x?

a) $\dfrac{x}{4}$ b) $\dfrac{x^2}{2}$ c) $\dfrac{\sqrt{x}}{4}$ d) $4\sqrt{x}$ e) $2\sqrt{x}$

Step 1: Making up numbers that fit

Suppose we let $x = 4$. It's a nice, easy number, it is not 0, 1 or 2, and if the square has an area of 4, it will be easy to find the length of each side, which we will probably have to do later.

Step 2: Using our number to answer their question

Well, if the area of the square is 4, then each side of the square is 2 (because $\sqrt{4} = 2$) and then the perimeter is the sum of all four sides, so 2+2+2+2=8. And that's my answer: 8

Step 3: Substitute our number into their choices, looking to see which one matches our answer

Let's see: my answer is 8, and I got that answer when I used $x = 4$. So when I try the answers…

a) $\dfrac{4}{4} = 1$ **NO** b) $\dfrac{4^2}{2} = 8$ **YES!** c) $\dfrac{\sqrt{4}}{4} = \dfrac{2}{4}$ **NO** d) $4\sqrt{4} = 4 \times 2 = 8$ **YES!** e) $2\sqrt{4} = 2 \times 2 = 4$ **NO**

Oh, NO! We have two that match my answer. OK, back to Step 1…

Well, if we let x=9, then each side of the square is now 3, and the perimeter 12.
So now, my answer is 12 and I used x = 9. Now I just have to recheck choices B and D...

b) $\dfrac{9^2}{2} = 40.5$ **NO**   **d)** $4\sqrt{9} = 4 \times 3 = 12$ **YES!**

Boy! It's a good thing we checked all of the answers. If we had stopped after finding the first match, we would have had the wrong answer. Phew!

Let's do another...

If $p + r + 1 = n^2$, then which of the following is the average (arithmetic mean) of p and r?

a) $\dfrac{(n+1)(n-1)}{2}$ **b)** $\dfrac{n^2+1}{2}$ **c)** $2n^2-1$ **d)** $\dfrac{(n-1)^2}{2}$ **e** $2(1-n)^2$

This time, let's have you work through the method with me...

1. Make up numbers for p, r, and n.

p =	r =	n =

Wait! Do your numbers fit the question?

Add $p + r + 1$. Do you get n^2? If so, great. If not, you need to fix your numbers.

> Are you stuck? It might be that you are making up the numbers in the wrong order! Try picking a value for *n* first. Just about anything will do. I'll say $n = 6$. So $n^2 = 36$. Now, I just have to pick *p* and *r* so that $p + r + 1 = 36$. There are LOTS of easy ways.. I'll say p = 30, r = 5. See how it works? Now, don't just use my numbers – go find your own, starting with n.

(I'll just pause to let everybody catch up...hmmm...ok, that's enough)

Now, in step 2, we answer their question: we find the average of p and r, but we use the numbers we chose for p and r. For example, since my numbers were p = 30 and r = 5, when I find their average, I get (30 + 5)/2 = 17.5, which is MY answer. (You probably got a different answer because you used different numbers.)

Finally, it's step 3: I'm going to substitute n=6 into the answer choices. You do the same with your value of n. Here's what I get:

a) $\dfrac{(6+1)(6-1)}{2} = \dfrac{7 \times 5}{2} = 17.5$ **YES**

b) $\dfrac{6^2+1}{2} = \dfrac{37}{2} = 18.5$ **NO**

c) $2 \times 6^2 - 1 = 71$ **NO**

d) $\dfrac{(6-1)^2}{2} = \dfrac{25}{2} = 12.5$ **NO**

e) $2(1-6)^2 = 2(-5) = 50$ **NO**

Taa-daa! [*] Now you try a few…

___

[*] Like the National Football League, ETS frowns on trash-talking, gloating or taunting. But when you take an annoying algebra problem like this one and reduce it to a simple game of calculator arithmetic—well, it's hard not to gloat. Maybe it's even worth a ten-yard penalty.

Practice Set #2: Back Door Problems

1. If $x = \dfrac{y}{2}$ then $2y - \dfrac{x}{2} = ?$

a) $5y$ b) $4y$ c) $2y$ d) $\dfrac{5}{4}y$ e) $\dfrac{7}{4}y$

2. Lucy can wrap n candies per minute. The candies are then packed into boxes of 12. Which of the following expressions is equal to the number of boxes worth of candy that Lucy can wrap in w hours?

a) $\dfrac{nw}{12}$ b) $\dfrac{nw}{5}$ c) $5nw$ d) $12nw$ e) $72nw$

3. If $2x = 3y = 6z$, then the average of x and $y =$

a) $2.5z$ b) $3z$ c) $5z$ d) $5.5z$ e) $11z$

4. If m teaspoons of powdered concentrate are needed to make $3p$ ounces of lemonade, then $m+2$ teaspoons will be enough to make how many ounces of lemonade, of the same strength?

a) $3p + 2$ b) $3p + 6$ c) $\dfrac{3pm}{m+2}$ d) $\dfrac{3m}{(m+2)p}$ e) $\dfrac{3p(m+2)}{m}$

5. A container can hold a maximum of L gallons of water. It is initially 3/5 full. Then, after x gallons are removed, the remainder is divided equally into two smaller containers. How many gallons go into each of the smaller containers?

a) $\dfrac{3}{5}L - 2x$ b) $\dfrac{3}{10}L - \dfrac{x}{2}$ c) $\dfrac{3}{5}L - x$ d) $\dfrac{6}{5}L - x$ e) $\dfrac{6}{5}L - \dfrac{x}{2}$

6. If $\dfrac{1}{4a} = b$ and $\dfrac{1}{4b} = c$ then $\dfrac{c}{a} = ?$

a) 1 b) 4 c) 16 d) $4c^2$ e) $4/c$

Set #2 Answer Key

For each of these problems, the first thing I'll show you is the numbers that I made up for the variables. In some cases, you can use the first numbers that pop into your head. Other times, you have to think for a while. If you couldn't come up with your own numbers, look and see what numbers I used. Then, go back to the problem to see if you can finish it from there yourself. But if not, continue with the explanation given in the key below.

1. We can use $y = 10$ and $x = 5$…(There's nothing special about these—they were the first I thought of.)

With those numbers, the answer to the question is $2y - \dfrac{x}{2} = 2 \times 10 - \dfrac{5}{2} = 17.5$

Then, when we substitute $y = 10$ into each answer choice, the only one that matches is e) $\dfrac{7}{4} \times 10 = 17.5$.

ANSWER: e

2. We can use $n = 10$ and $w = 3$…(Again, nothing special about these.)

With those numbers, then Lucy can wrap 10 per minute x 60 minutes in an hour = 600 candies in an hour. So in 3 hours, she can wrap 600 x 3 = 1800 candies. And they are packed in boxes of 12, so 1800/12 = 150 boxes.

Now we put our $n = 10$ and $w = 3$ into each answer choice. The only one that matches is c) $5nw = 5 \times 10 \times 3 = 150$.
ANSWER: c

3. OK, this one requires a little more effort to come up with numbers that fit. You might have an easier time if you make up z first. For example, if you choose z=5 then 6z=30. Now you have to choose y = 10 (so that 3y=30) and you have to choose x = 15 (so that 2x=30). So now we have our numbers: z=5, y=10 and x = 15…

With those numbers, the average of x and y is (10+15)/2=12.5

And then we substitute z=5 into the answer choices and the only match is choice a) 2.5z = 2.5 x 5 = 12.5
ANSWER: a

4. After you replace the variables with numbers, this is just a ratio problem (See page ___ for help with ratios.) So say we use m=5 and p=6.

Now the problem reads as follows:
If 5 (remember: m = 5) teaspoons of concentrate are needed to make 18 (because 3p=3x6=18) ounces of lemonade, then 7 (that's m+2=5+2=7) teaspoons will enough to make how many ounces? This is a ratio problem:

$\dfrac{5}{18} = \dfrac{7}{x}$, cross multiply, divide, get x=25.2…yuck. But don't lose heart! Continue the process.

Now substitute m=5 and p=6 into each answer choice. Use your calculator! If you are careful, you will discover that choice e) $\dfrac{3p(m+2)}{m} = \dfrac{3 \times 6(5+2)}{5} = 25.2$ is the one and only match! How about that.

ANSWER: e

5. Some possible numbers are L = 50 and x = 6…

If you want to be lazy here (and don't we always?) you should pick an L that is easy to take 3/5 of. That's why I chose L = 50. So the container originally held 3/5 of 50 which is 30 gallons. Then, for x, you can pick anything less than 30. I chose 6. That leaves 24 gallons. Divided in half, it will be 12 in each tank.

Then, check each answer choice and you will find that only choice   b) $\dfrac{3}{10}L - \dfrac{x}{2} = \dfrac{3}{10} \times 50 - \dfrac{6}{2} = 12$ is a match.

ANSWER: b

6. This one looks harder than it is. But you might need your calculator to help you find numbers that ft. For example, suppose you pick a=10. Then $b = \dfrac{1}{40} = .025$. And then $c = \dfrac{1}{4 \times .025} = \dfrac{1}{.1} = 10$. So now we have our three numbers: a=10, b=.025 and c=10…

Now answer their question: $\dfrac{c}{a} = \dfrac{10}{10} = 1$. (See how easy that was? When it's harder to find numbers that fit, then the actual question is always pretty easy.)

And finally, we check the answer choices. Obviously, 'a' matches, but be careful to check all of them in case others match too. But they don't. So we're done.
ANSWER: a

Memo: The well-meant words that do you harm:

"I'm not a good test-taker."

I hear it so many times. Students tell me that they are not good test-takers. Actually, I hear it the most from their parents. I know these parents mean well, but they are not helping the cause. It has got to stop. Parents: stop saying it. Students: stop listening to it. From this day on, let there be no such thing as "a bad-test taker".

I understand why parents say these things to their children. From early in school, progress is measured and grades are assigned primarily by testing. If parents feel that their child is an intelligent, hard-working kid, but the test results disagree, "not-a-good-test-taker" is a gentle explanation. And their belief that there is more to you than tests reveal is, of course, absolutely true – it's true for all of us! But making some official-sounding diagnosis that you are not a good test taker is completely unjustified and unproductive.

There is no such thing as a person who is good at taking all tests or bad at taking all tests. "Bad-test-taker-itis" is not some disease that you catch (or inherit) and it is not a permanent condition. You need to stop believing in it. If you believe you are a bad test-taker, it will affect how you take tests. It becomes a self-fulfilling prophecy. Believing it makes it come true. Here's how it happens. There comes a point in every test where you encounter adversity. (Oooh, "adversity". Is that an SAT word? It means difficulty or hardship. So when I say you encounter adversity, I mean that things aren't going too well.) A problem confuses you. Another takes too long. A third one requires you to take a guess. These things are all NORMAL! They happen to just about EVERYONE! But if you believe that you are a "bad test-taker", you go through a downward spiral of anxiety and doubt. *"Oh, no. It's not going well now. I knew this would happen. This always happens to me. This is why I am not a good test taker."* And so it goes. (By the way, this is yet another reason why the non-conformist who cuts corners and copies your math homework is beating your SAT score. He doesn't go through the spiral of anxiety and doubt--he doesn't care! So he ends up using his time better, spending none of it on SAT angst. And then he beats your score. I'm telling you, we can learn a lot from this kid.)

But some of you already believe that you are not good test-takers. You are reading this and thinking, "Well, he's just wrong, because I really am a bad test-taker". How can I help you to change your belief? Let me tell you another joke. (My students all LOVE my jokes. Really.)

A man walks into his doctor's office with a fork sticking out of his ear, a spoon up his nose, and a slice of pizza taped to his armpit. And the doctor says: I know what your problem is-- You're not eating right.

Now, what's the point? Well first of all, we don't care if you are a good test taker in the bigger cosmic sense. All we care about is: are you good at taking the math SAT? And, up until now, the answer may have been "no", but there has been a reason: you haven't been doing it right. So your test anxiety has not been a sign of some deep psychological disorder. It has been a rational response to your situation. You have to take this giant scary test that will play a big part in determining where you go to college, and YOU HAVE NO IDEA HOW TO DO IT! You should be anxious! Imagine if you had to take your driver's road test with as little knowledge or preparation as the average student has for the SAT. You'd be pretty anxious. And I bet it wouldn't go too well. But it would NOT be because you are "not a good test-taker." You've just never been taught the right way. And the right way is much easier than the wrong way.

So here's the plan: you read this book, you learn the right way, you PRACTICE what you have learned and then, for at least this one stupid test, you are a GREAT test-taker. The world's best. Does this mean you won't hit any turbulence? No, it doesn't. Everybody hits rough spots. But you'll stay calm. You can say: " I did it in practice, I can do it now. I know what I'm doing."

LESSON #4: The Grid-Ins

There is something strange about this section. It should be the section that students like the most and also the one in which they score highest. After all, it is most like the tests you take in school. And yet, it has been my experience that students find this section vaguely discomfiting ("discomfiting"—another high-power vocabulary word. Go look it up.) More importantly, students often do less well on this section than they do on the test overall. But the Grid-ins are easier when you've learned a few tricks.

And even better, they are tricks that you already have seen: Trial and Error and the Back Door play. These methods both work even when there are no answer choices to choose from. They just have to be adapted slightly, in ways that I will show you soon. But first, I need to address one of the most commonly repeated pieces of BAD SAT ADVICE:

"Always answer all of the Grid-ins because there is no penalty for getting them wrong."

This is WRONG. It is an example of BAD ADVICE. Here's why:

People who tell you there is no penalty for getting the Grid-ins wrong do not understand the SAT. They are right when they say that you do not lose points. But they have forgotten the other penalty that you learned about in Lesson #1—the waste of TIME. Like every other math section, the grid-ins are arranged in order of difficulty. The last 2 or 3 are nasty. Don't waste time on them unless they are part of the Game Plan you mapped out in Lesson #1.

And, now, on to the tricks!

Trial and Error in the Grid-In Section

Read the following problem carefully (which is, of course, the ONLY way to read!) and when you are sure you understand what they are asking for, TAKE A GUESS at the answer.

You have only dimes and quarters in your pocket and there are 4 more dimes than quarters. If the total value of the coins is $3.55, how many quarters do you have?

Your Guess:

Do not look at the next page until you have written your guess in the box.

The most important thing about your guess is NOT whether it is right or wrong. We'll get to that later. The most important thing is that you did in fact take a guess. (And if you still have not guessed, go back and do it NOW!) And your guess should not have taken that long to come up with – maybe 5 or 10 seconds at the most. If you took longer than that, it's because you were not just trying to guess – you were trying to guess <u>correctly</u>. This is another place where the non-conformist has an edge: when it comes time to guess, he just throws out the first number he thinks of. "Good" students do not often have to take guesses because they were paying attention when the teacher taught the "right" way to do the problem. This makes them good students but timid at guessing. Just be bold! Just take a guess! See where it leads.

So let's get back to the last problem. I (obviously) don't know what you guessed, so let's say that your first guess was 10 quarters. (It was? Really? Talk about coincidences...) Now what do you do? The exact same process as when the problem had answer choices:

Is it 10 quarters? If it is, then there are also 14 dimes.
10 quarters are worth $2.50 and 14 dimes are worth $1.40
Together, they are worth $2.50 +$1.40 = $3.90 which is too much.

So let's guess a smaller number of quarters. Maybe it's 8 quarters.
Is it 8? Then there are also 12 dimes.
8 quarters are worth $2.00 and 12 dimes are worth $1.20
and together they are worth $2.00 +$1.20 = $3.20 which is too small.

I bet it's 9! If there are 9 quarters, there are 13 dimes.
9 quarters are worth $2.25 and 13 dimes are worth $1.30
and together they are worth $2.25 + $1.30 = $3.55 which is CORRECT!

See? That wasn't so hard. You just have to jump in and take a guess. Let's do a few more...

A rectangle's length is three times as long as its width. If the area of the rectangle is 48, what is the perimeter?

Just start making up rectangles! Make their lengths three times the widths. I'll even draw some rectangles for you:

I'd rather that you pick the numbers, but if you can't get started, I'll take the first guess:

Suppose the width is 10. Then the length is 30. So the area is 300. Nope, too big.

When you find the numbers that make the area equal to 48, write them down. And then add up all four sides to find the perimeter. (You should get 32.)

Here are a few more for you to try. The answers are on the next page. And remember, with trial and error, the answer is the solution. You just keep playing until you find numbers that work!

Practice Set #3: Trial and Error in the Grid-Ins

1. The product of two consecutive integers is 15 more than the larger of the two integers. Find the smaller of the two consecutive integers.

2. Water pours into a tank at a rate of 16 gallons per minute until the tank is full. Then, the tank is drained at a rate of 20 gallons per minute until it is empty. If the tank drains 12 minutes FASTER than it filled, how many gallons does it hold?

3. One third of a number is two more than half of the number. What is the number?

4. Given that $(2^x)^x = 512$, what is the value of 2^x?

5. Team A has 15 boys and 3 girls. Team B has 5 boys and 7 girls. The two teams trade players, Team A sending boys to Team B, while Team B sends an equal number of girls back to Team A, until the ratio of boys to girls is the same for both teams. At that point, a total of how many players will have changed teams?

6. The average of n consecutive even integers is 5 more than the first of them. Find n.

Set #3: Answer Key

1. Just start multiplying consecutive integers, see what happens:
2x3=6, 6 is not 15 more than 3
4x5=20, 20 IS 5 more than 5…And that's it! But they want the smaller of the two so…
ANSWER: 4

2. Start with a nice round number, easy to divide...say 160 gallons. Then filling takes 160/16=10 minutes, emptying takes 160/20=8 minutes. Difference is only 2, not 12. Not big enough. In fact, since we want the difference to be 6 times as big as 2, now I'll try a number 6 times as big as my first guess: 960 gallons. 960/16=60 minutes, 960/20=48 minutes, and the difference is now 12 minutes. Done.
ANSWER: 960

3. Take a guess, let's say 9. A third of 9 is 3, half of 9 is 4.5. But 3 is not 2 more than 4.5. In fact, it's less. How can a third be more than a half? Oh, wait…negative numbers! Say -12…A third is -4 and half is -6. And -4 is 2 more than -6. Got it.
ANSWER: -12

4. Get out your calculator and try some numbers. When you try $(2^3)^3$, you'll get 512. So x=3 and 2^3=8
ANSWER: 8

5. This is easier with a chart:

TEAM A: TEAM B:

BBBBBBBBBBBBBBB   BBBBB
GGG   GGGGGGG

Now, just start by moving a boy from A to B and a girl from B to A. Are the ratios the same? No, not yet. So move another. And another. When you've moved 3 boys to team B and 3 girls to team A, Team A will have 12 boys and 6 girls, which is a 2: 1 ratio. And team B will have 8 boys and 4 girls, which is also a 2:1 ratio. And the total number of players to change teams will be 3+3=6.
ANSWER: 6

6. Let's try 5 consecutive even integers: 10, 12, 14, 16, 18. The average is 14 which is 4 more than the first of them. So now let's try 6 numbers instead: 10, 12, 14, 16, 18…add them up, divide by 6, and you get 15. And 15 is 5 more than 10, which was the first of the numbers. So we are done.
ANSWER: 6

The Back Door Trick in the Grid-In Section

Just like trial and error, the Back Door play also works in the Grid-Ins, even though at first look, you might think that it isn't possible. After all, the basic idea behind the Back Door play is that after you get your answer using your numbers, you go around *to the answer choices* and substitute your numbers to see which answer matches. (I am assuming you have already read Lesson #3.) So if there are no answer choices, you can't use this method, right? Wrong!

You CAN still make up numbers that fit the problem. And you CAN still use those numbers to answer their question. You just can't do the third step, where you put your numbers into the answer choices. And here's the good news: YOU DON'T NEED TO DO THE THIRD STEP! Just take whatever answer you came up with and enter it into the grid. That's it. You're done!

This often leaves students feeling surprised and a little nervous: *"That's it? That's all I have to do? But I just made up those numbers. How do I know they are right?"* Well, I can answer that question, but first I want to look at three examples:

*　　　　　　　　*　　　　　　　　*

The average of x and y is twice as big as the average of a, b and c.

What is the value of $\dfrac{x+y}{a+b+c}$?

Suppose we make up numbers that fit what they say.
I'm going to pick a = 5, b = 10, c = 15 because its easy to get their average, which is 10.
Then, I'll need the average of x and y to be twice that, which is 20. So I'll pick x = 15, y = 25.
(For more help making up numbers to fit average problems, see page 80.)

OK, then using my numbers to calculate $\dfrac{x+y}{a+b+c}$, I get $\dfrac{15+25}{5+10+15} = \dfrac{40}{30} = \dfrac{4}{3}$ which I can grid in as a fraction, just as it is, or change to a decimal (but why bother?). Either way, I'm done.

*　　　　　　　　*　　　　　　　　*

If n is a factor of 12 and p is a factor of 20, and $1 < n < p < 20$, and q = p/n, where q is an integer, find one possible value of q.

And again, we make up numbers…
Factors of 12 are 1, 2, 3, 4, 6, and 12—but we need an n that is greater than 1.
Factors of 20 are 1, 2, 4, 5, 10, and 20—but p is less than 20.
Since p/n has to be an integer, let's use p = 10 and n = 2…we get q = 10/2 = 5.
So we enter it into the grid and move on to the next question.

*　　　　　　　　*　　　　　　　　*

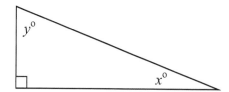

If $4x = y$, what is $y - x$?

Once again, we try to make up numbers that fit…in this case, that means the angles of the triangle have to add up to $180°$, so x and y have to add up to 90.

Let's try $x = 30$, $y = 60$. But wait—y has to be 4 times x. 60 is not 4 times 30. Ok, try again:

How about $x = 20$, $y = 70$…nope.

How about $x = 15$, $y = 75$…no, and now we've gone too far.

Ok, how about $x = 18$, $y = 72$…let's see...adds up to 90… $4 \times 18 = 72$ …Ok, these numbers fit. Now what do they want? Oh, $y - x$…well with my numbers, that's $72 - 18 = 54$. And we are done!

*   *   *

Now, let's take a look at the bigger picture. The three examples that we just worked through were chosen to give you some practice, but also to make a point. Together, they answer the question, "How do I know I am right?" It turns out that when you make up numbers that fit the problem, there are three possibilities about what's going on behind the scenes:

i. Yes, you just made up some numbers. You could have made up others, but you would have landed on the same answer anyway. So don't worry, and enter your answer in the grid.

Or…

ii. You just made up some numbers. You could have made up others and you would have landed on a different answer. But that's OK. There can be more than one right answer to a grid-in problem. You have found one of them. One is enough. So don't worry, and enter your answer in the grid.

Or…

iii. You just made up some numbers. And, whether you realize it or not, the numbers you have selected are the ONLY ones that can possibly fit the problem. So yours is the only right answer. Don't worry, and enter your answer in the grid.

Do you see a recurring theme here?

Make up numbers that fit. Get an answer. Enter it. And don't worry.

On the next page, there's another handful for practice.

Practice Set #4: Back Door Grid-Ins

1. For all $y \neq 0$, $\dfrac{(4+y)^2 - (4-y)^2}{y} = ?$

2. When q is increased by $r\%$, the resulting value is more than $3q$ and less than $3.5q$.   Find one possible value of r.

3. The average of a, b and c is 2. What is the value of $2^{(a+b+c)}$?

4. Point P has coordinates (0,3). Point Q has coordinates (x,y) and the slope of segment PQ is ¼.
    Find the value of $\dfrac{4y - 12}{x}$.

5. The circumference of the outer circle is how much greater than that of the inner circle?

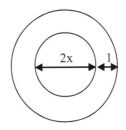

6. What is the area of the shaded region?

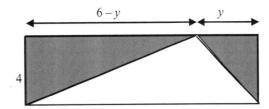

59

Set #4: Answer Key

1. Pick ANY value you want for y. Then, use your calculator. So, let's say y=5...

Then, $\dfrac{(4+y)^2-(4-y)^2}{y} = \dfrac{(4+5)^2-(4-5)^2}{5} = \dfrac{(9)^2-(-1)^2}{5} = \dfrac{80}{5} = 16\ldots$ and you are done. But if you don't believe me, go ahead and try another number for y. You'll still get the same answer.
ANSWER: 16

2. We have to make up q and r so that they fit the problem. So if I pick q=10 then I have to pick r so that increasing 10 by r% gives an answer between 30 (which is 3q) and 35 (which is 3.5q). I know that if you increase 10 by 100% you get 20. And by 200% gives you 30. Increase it by 300% and you'll get 40 which is to big. I need a number between 200% and 250%. I pick 210. You can pick other values, as long as they are in that range.
ANSWER: Anything greater than 200 and less than 250

3. Once again, we have to make up numbers that fit. Since I want the average of a, b and c to be 2, the numbers I choose are 2, 2 and 2. (Can you just do that? Yes you can. See page ___).
Then $2^{(a+b+c)} = 2^{(2+2+2)} = 2^6 = 64$. And you are done.
ANSWER: 64

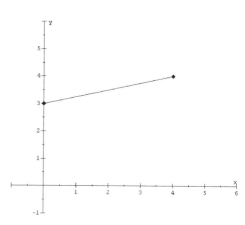

4. Making up possible values for x and y is a little harder this time. Start with a neat diagram. We know where point P is. And point Q must be somewhere so that the slope, or rise over run = ¼ . For example, we could go up 1 and over 4. If we do, the point we land on is (4,4) so we use x=4 and y=4.

Now, we can answer the question: $\dfrac{4y-12}{x} = \dfrac{4\times4-12}{4} = \dfrac{4}{4} = 1$ and that's the answer. And yes, there are other values for x and y that we could have chosen. But we'd get the same answer.
ANSWER: 1

5. Pick any value for x. I'll say x = 4. So 2x = 8, which is the diameter of the inner circle. So its radius is 4 and its circumference is 8π. Then the bigger circle has a radius of 5 and a circumference of 10π. The difference is 2π. (But you can't grid in π, so you change it to a decimal and grid in the approximate answer instead.)
ANSWER: 6.2832

6. As soon as you make up a value for y, this is just the area of 2 triangles, each with a height of 4. For example, if we use y=2, then the shaded triangle on the left has area ½ 4x4=8 and the one on the right is ½ 2x4=4, which makes the total area 12. And that's what you get no matter what y-value you choose.
ANSWER: 12

Lesson # 5: "When Should I Guess?"—And Advice on your Attitude

My physics students have to put up with this all the time: they ask a simple question, hoping for a brief answer, and they get a long, involved answer instead. And at the end, I have to ask them, "Did I answer your question? Or was it more of answer than you hoped for?" But it's not my fault. Yes, I am naturally long-winded, but some questions are not as simple as they seem to be. This is one of them.

The Simple Answer (which is WRONG):

> When you can eliminate one or more of the answer choices as incorrect, you should then guess from the remaining choices.

That is the answer you have probably been given. To understand why this is wrong, you really have to understand why so many people believe that it's right.

Suppose you are in the section where the questions have 5 answer choices and you guess randomly on a bunch of them. You have a one in five chance of guessing right, which would earn you a point. But on each of the four that you get wrong, you will lose a quarter of a point and, in theory, you will break even. (That is why they say that random guessing is not likely to change your score.)

But now suppose that you were able to eliminate ONE of the wrong answers before you took you guess. Now, with only 4 answer choices remaining, you have a one-in-four chance of guessing right. So, at least in theory, you will get one right out of every four times you guess, and then get the other three wrong, thus losing only ¾ of a point. So you come out <u>slightly</u> ahead.

Doesn't that sound reasonable? How can it be wrong? Well, it is wrong, and for at least THREE reasons:

1. While you are taking the test, you can't be certain that the answer you have eliminated is really wrong! After all, you are not feeling too certain about this problem, or you would not be guessing. But the calculation above assumes that you never accidentally exclude the right answer when you guess. If you accidentally ruled out the CORRECT answer, you have lost the slight edge that this guessing strategy claims to give you.[*]

2. The SAT is not an all-night casino, where you can keep betting for as long as you can stay awake, hoping to parlay some slight perceived advantage into a big take-home payoff. The laws of probability are really just approximations and they only work when you are dealing with large samples. BUT YOU SHOULD ONLY HAVE TO GUESS ON A SMALL HANDFUL OF PROBLEMS! So the fact that some particular guessing strategy might offer a ¼ point advantage for every 5 questions guessed is irrelevant (even if it were true, which it is not). If you are guessing a lot, you probably did not read Lesson #1 and you are still answering too many questions.

---

[*] Remember, we are not playing "Who wants to be a millionaire?" where the wrong answers are magically whisked away when you choose a 50-50. YOU have to eliminate them. And you COULD be wrong.

3. The argument ignores the hidden penalty for getting things wrong – the time you have wasted. After all, since random guessing isn't supposed to change your score, why not answer everything? I'll tell you why not: IT"S A WASTE OF TIME! The time you spend trying to eke out a slight guessing edge should be spent getting other problems right!

"So get to the answer already! When should I guess?"

(I warned you that this was going to be a long answer.)

The reason you don't want to guess on every question is that it is a waste of time. But what if you have already spent time on the question? In that case, you have already invested the time and you can't get it back anyway. Isn't it likely that you have had some tiny glimmer of understanding? Your chances of getting it right are surely better than they would be if you guessed randomly. After all, if the problem you are working on is within your Answer Zone, it's because your track record shows that you have a reasonable shot at getting it right. Otherwise, it wouldn't be worth spending time on and it wouldn't' be in your Answer Zone, like a long jump shot that isn't worth shooting. (If you don't know what I am talking about, please go back and read Lesson #1.)

Which brings us to the answer you have been waiting for:

THE ONLY RATIONAL GUESSING STRATEGY IN THE UNIVERSE

If you are working in your Answer Zone and you have already spent time on the question, GO FOR IT! Take your best guess. You have already invested the time. Now go ahead and take your best shot.

HOWEVER, you should not misinterpret this advice as a justification for answering too many questions. If you follow the right Game Plan, you should NOT have to guess too often.

Also, DO NOT worry about whether you have ruled out a sufficient number of "wrong" answers. If you have a clue, a hunch, an inkling, the slightest leaning…GO FOR IT!

This is part of a larger idea, about when to be aggressive and when to be cautious. It all goes back to those awful experimental sections that you are subjected to. You have to remember the reason they make you take those sections: to evaluate questions for possible future use. The experimental section is their key to continuity between older versions of the SAT and new ones. When a question appears at the end of an SAT section that counts, it is because when it appeared in an experimental section, two things happened:

1. A low percentage of students got the problem right.

2. The students who got it right were the ones who were scoring higher.

On the other hand, when most of the students answer a problem from the experimental section correctly, including those students who are scoring low, then that problem gets placed toward the front of the section. So the position of a problem in the test is like a historical record of how well students did on that problem in the past, when it first appeared on experimental sections. When you understand that, you can take a big step forward. You can approach the test in a more sophisticated, sneakier way.

How do you use this information? You let it affect your attitude as you move through the test. [*]

At the beginning of each section, you should be aggressive and bold:

Trust your instincts and don't omit anything. After all, if a problem appears early in the section, then you know that students just like you were able to answer it correctly when it first appeared on an experimental section. So, if you are stuck, it's not time to think harder, it's time to think DIFFERENTLY! Play, draw a diagram, make up a number, take a guess. OR go back and read the question again, because you may have missed something obvious. But the overall point that I am trying to make is that if a problem appears early in the section, it CANNOT BE THAT HARD!! So, as the educators at the Nike Company might say, JUST DO IT! Even if you have to guess.

As you move to the harder questions, you should be more cautious and selective:

As you approach the end of your zone, you encounter questions that gave students more trouble in the past (when they appeared on the experimental sections). So be alert and be cautious. The answer that seems obvious here is probably wrong. And if you come to a problem that completely overwhelms you, you'd be better off leaving it alone than investing the time it would take to guess.

There. Have I answered your question? Or was that more of an answer than you were hoping for?

---

[*] I am working on putting this concept into a song, taking my inspiration from the *School House Rock* classics such as *Conjunction Junction, What's Your Function* and *I'm Just a Bill*. My working title is *I'm Number Twenty* and so far, the lyrics I have are:

I'm Question Number Twenty, you know where to find me
Question Number Twenty - Nasty as can be
I started out on an experimental section
And everybody got me wrong, oh yeah
Everybody got me wrong, so watch out now.
Everybody got me wrong.

This song has been performed in public to great acclaim. I expect to hear from the Public Television people any day now.

Memo: Testing with Extended Time

Q. Which techniques apply to you?

A. All of them!

This note is for those students who test with extended time. If that's you, you should read the lesson and follow the time budget it contains. But before you read this lesson, if you have not already read Lesson #1, please go back and read it. If you think that time management is not important for you because you have all this extra time to play with, you are mistaken. You have an extra 90 minutes. You should use that time wisely. So begin by reading Lesson #1, "It's About Time".

How do I get extra time on the SAT?

To test with extended time, first of all, you have to request it. But you don't get it just for asking. Extended time is an accommodation offered in response to a diagnosed disability that would put you at a disadvantage if you didn't have more time. In most cases, we are talking about a learning disability such as dyslexia or attention deficit disorder. In general, if for any reason you are usually given extra time to take tests in school, you <u>may</u> also be able to get extended time on the SAT. In particular…

or

you have a "504" plan or an Individualized Educational Plan (IEP) that specifies extended time for testing;

or

you are a "classified" student, receiving special services from your school district;

you have been evaluated by a certified professional (usually an educational psychologist);

then you <u>may</u> be eligible to test with extended time. To find out, you have to apply. There is a form that you fill out and send to ETS, and then there is a form that they send back. If you think you want to do this, get started soon. Go see your guidance counselor tomorrow and get the ball rolling. It can take few weeks (and possibly longer, if there is a conflict over your application).

On the other hand, if you've never heard of any of this, then it probably does not apply to you and you can skip this section.

"Why would I want extended time? The SAT is already long enough…"

Well, of course, that's true. The SAT is an ordeal even at three and a half hours. And now, I am telling you that if you ask nicely, and your paperwork is in order, they will let you extend the ordeal by another hour and a half. Why would any sane person do that? There can only be one reason. Pay close attention, because it is a very good reason:

If you use the extended time properly, you will score higher

Oh, yeah. Did you forget? That's the whole point. But most students who get the extended time don't use it well, making one of two common mistakes: not spreading extra the time around evenly and not using enough of it. The first mistake is caused by guilt. The second mistake is caused by a lack of planning. Let's try to fix both of those problems.

Using Extended Time Properly

Step 1: Stop Feeling Guilty! Use EVERY minute!

Whenever I work with a student who has taken an SAT with extended time, the first question I ask is: "How much of the extended time did you use?" And students always tell me that they "only used a little of it". This is always said with a hint of apology about using any extra time and pride that they didn't need much. I've never met a student who answered, "I used EVERY minute. They had to rip the answer sheet out of my hands and drag me from the room kicking and screaming!" I've come to believe that all of the kids who get extra time feel guilty for having it.[*] This might be because in school, when you get extra time on a history test, some of your friends might tease you, or worse, complain about you, saying the magic words: "It's not fair!" And secretly, you agree with them. You think that you are being given an unfair advantage, so you don't want to take unreasonable advantage of it.

Now, stop listening to your friends, and listen to me instead. About that guilt: GET OVER IT! Having extra time is NOT unfair. Of course it's not fair either. NOTHING about the SAT is fair or unfair. Haven't you been paying attention? The whole system is bizarre. Fairness has nothing to do with it. But you did not write the rules. You should not feel guilty about playing by the rules. And if this one time, you caught a lucky break, well it's about time. Now make the most of it. Use EVERY extra minute they give you and use it right. I'll show you how.

Step 2: Follow a "Time Budget" that forces you to spread the time out evenly.

NOTE: As of the most recent SAT changes (March 2005), you should NOT have to do this yourself. If you are given 50% more time, you are supposed to be in a separate room from the rest of the students where a proctor is supposed to time each section for you so that you MUST spend your extra time evenly. This is a good thing – it means that you just have to keep working until they tell you to stop.

And now, the most commonly asked question about extra time:

"Since I have more time, should I at least try some more of the hard questions?"

NO, NO, NO! Double NO! Triple NO. NO. Well, maybe.

Before I can explain the answer to this question, I have to ask you one: Have you read Lesson #1, yet? It IS about time, and if you have not read it, you're missing the point. We'll still be here when you get back. Go read it, now!

*   *   *

OK, now I can explain:

You just have <u>extended</u> time. You don't have <u>unlimited</u> time. And you definitely do not have unlimited energy. Getting things wrong is a waste of time, no matter how much time you have. And spending time on problems you can't solve is frustrating and demoralizing. So it still does not make any sense to work on hard questions that you don't need to reach your score goal. You should still find the Game Plan that matches your score goal and stick to it. When you reach your score goal on a practice test, you choose the next goal and follow that Game Plan instead.

But I did say "maybe"…

If you do find yourself with a few extra minutes, and you have studied Lesson #3, The Back Door, then you can scan the end of the sections looking for back door problems. But other than that, stay in your zone and follow your time budget.

One last note of optimism:

You should know that some of the most dramatic score improvements I have seen have come from those students who test with extended time. One of my students went from a 380 to a 540 after just two lessons with me. And another went from the mid 400's to the high 600's. Part of the improvement comes from following the game plan, but I think that there's more to it. In many cases, the reason for the extra time is ADD. But the good news about the math SAT is that it does NOT require a long attention span. Each question is its own little puzzle game that you work on for just a minute or two. And then you move on. (In comparison, students with ADD find the reading comprehension to be a kind of torture. Actually, almost every student feels that way.)

My point is that if you are a special needs student, if you have a 504 plan or an IEP, then it is not unlikely that you occasionally have had a rough time of it in school. You may be dreading the SAT as yet another experience that is sure to bring you down. Let me give you some hope—you could easily surprise yourself. Just remember to concentrate on remaining calm as you follow your game plan:

Go slowly.
Use all of your time.
Don't work on problems that are harder than what you need to reach your score goal.
Play with each question

THIS IS NOT SCHOOL!

PART II: Actual Math – The ESSENTIAL SAT Topics

Well, you've seen the tricks and that is half the battle, but only half. The rest of your score increase comes from reviewing the mathematical concepts that frequently appear on the SAT. If you have already completed Algebra I and Geometry, then most of this will be familiar to you. In fact, the last time you saw a bunch of these was back in middle school. Remainders, anyone?

With each explained concept, you will find some examples and some sample questions for you to try. And, of course, the best way for you to practice applying these ideas is to take more practice tests. You will find that some of these concepts show up on nearly every SAT (such as the counting principle, the made-up-symbol problem, and the shaded region problem), while others only show up occasionally. But remember, if as a result of mastering these concepts, you get 6 more right answers, you are looking at another 50-point increase.

Round 1 – Middle School Topics:

Math Vocabulary

Divisibility, Remainders and Pattern Problems

Mean, Median and Mode (and Average Problems the easy way)

Percents and Percent changes

Ratio problems

PRACTICE TEST ALERT: If you have worked through Part I and you understand Trial and Error and the Back Door Play, you are ready for another TIMED practice test (from *The Official SAT Study Guide*). Then, as you move through Part II, after each round of review, do another practice test. They should get easier each time.

Math Vocabulary Review

I'm sure that you once knew all of these terms, and you probably still know them now. But just in case…

Product: the answer when you multiply
Sum: the answer when you add
Quotient: the answer when you divide
Difference: the answer when you subtract

Integers: whole numbers and their additive inverses. Or, to put it in the language of students, "all the numbers and their negatives" such as –3, -2, -1, 0, 1, 2, 3…

Positive: GREATER than zero
Negative: LESS than zero
So zero not positive or negative. It's just zero.

Even integers: divisible by 2, such as 2 ,4 ,100 , …
Odd integers: not divisible by 2, such as 1, 3, 5, 2003…
Zero is EVEN.

Consecutive Integers: one after another such as 5,6,7,8…
Consecutive Even Integers: 2,4,6,8…
Consecutive Odd Integers: 3, 5, 7, 9, 11..

Multiples: the numbers you get when you multiply a given number by integers.
For example, some multiples of 6 are 6, 12, 18, 60, 600…

Factors: the integers that divide evenly into a given number.
For example, the factors of 12 are 1, 2, 3, 4, 6, and 12.

Prime Numbers: numbers that have only two factors: 1 and themselves.
Examples: 2, 3, 5, 7, 11, 13…
Note: 2 is the only EVEN prime number (because the other even numbers have 2 as a factor). Other than 2, the rest of the primes are odd. But not all odd numbers are prime. For example, 15 is odd but not prime (15 = 5x3).
And also note: 1 is not considered prime (don't worry about why not).

Set: for the purpose of the SAT, a set is just a bunch of numbers, often written between fancy brackets. For example, here is a set of 3 randomly chosen integers: {3,10, 190}

Units Digit: a fancy name for the ones column. So in the number 284, the units digit is a 4.

Remainders and Divisibility (and Pattern Problems)

Do you remember how to find a remainder? It's probably been a while. Try one now just to see if you can still do it:

What is the remainder when 101 is divided by 7?

In case you have forgotten, the remainder is NOT the same thing as the decimal part of your answer. If you don't know any tricks, you have no other choice but to do long division.

$$\begin{array}{r} 14 \\ 7{\overline{)101}} \\ \underline{7} \\ 31 \\ \underline{28} \\ 3 \end{array}$$

Of course, long division is a pain and it takes too long. You can avoid it if you have a calculator and you know what to do.

With a TI-34 II or Math Explorer Calculator:

These calculators have a feature called "integer divide". To use this feature, instead of pressing $\div$ (the divide button), you press $2^{nd} \div$. When you do this, the calculator automatically reports the answer in remainder form.

With ANY Calculator:

You can find out the remainder of a division problem by following this sequence:

1. Divide the two numbers
2. Drop the decimal from your answer and multiply by what you originally divided by
3. Subtract the end result from the original number

Let's try it with $101 \div 7$.

1. $101 \div 7 = 14.4285....$
2. Drop the decimal and we get 14. Then 14 x 7 = 98
3. $101 - 98 = 3$

So the remainder is 3. And of course, this matches what we got using long division.

Some common questions about this remainder-finding method...

Does it always work? Yes.

What if there is no remainder? Well, you will probably notice that when you divide the numbers, you don't get any decimal. But if you don't notice that, and you finish the procedure, the answer will be zero.

Why didn't they teach us this in middle school? I don't know.

How will this appear on the SAT? One of the most common ways is in a pattern problem.

Pattern Problems and Remainders:

> **If the sequence of letters "AEIOUXYZAEIOUXYZAEI..." continues indefinitely, what will be the 303rd letter in the sequence?**

This is actually a remainder question. There are 8 letters in the pattern and the pattern goes on for 303 letters. Find the remainder when 303 is divided by 8.

1. $303 \div 8 = 37.875$
2. Drop the decimal and multiply: $37 \times 8 = 296$.
3. Subtract: $303 - 296 = 7$ and that's the remainder.

So what is the answer? Well, you will get through the entire pattern 37 times and then have 7 leftover letters. Count off 7 letters into the pattern: A, E, I, O, U, X, <u>Y</u> and that's the answer!

There is one thing about this that sometimes tricks students. Suppose they had asked for the 168th letter in the pattern. In that case, the remainder is zero. So what is the answer—what is the 168th letter? (I'll let you think for a minute....)

The answer is "Z". If there is no remainder, it means that you finished the pattern with nothing left over. So the last letter in the pattern is the letter that you finished on.

I will give you a few more to practice with at the end of this section. But we are not done with remainders yet. You also need to learn how to make up numbers that fit remainder questions.

Making Up Numbers That Give You the Right Remainders:

Let's try one as a warm-up. I'm thinking of a number. You try to guess what it is. Here's a hint: when my number is divided by 6, the remainder is 2. Now try to guess what my number could be.

WRITE YOUR GUESS HERE. ☐

Don't look at the next page until you have taken a guess. And notice, I didn't say guess what my number IS, but rather what it COULD be. There are an infinite number of possibilities...

So what's the answer? And how do you find it?

Or did you find it? If not, do not feel bad. It has been a long time since you worked with remainders, and you may never have been asked to make up numbers that give you a certain remainder. It's just the kind of backwards twist that the SAT loves. Let's take a closer look:

We want a remainder of 2 when we divide by a number by 6. Of the many possible answers, here are some of the more commonly chosen ones:

$$14, \quad 20, \quad 26, \quad 38, \quad 62....$$

What these numbers have in common is that you can get them by choosing any multiple of 6 and then adding 2. For example:

$$14 = 12 + 2 = 6*2 + 2$$

and $\quad 20 = 18 + 2 = 6*3 + 2$

and $\quad 26 = 24 + 2 = 6*4 + 2$

and $\quad 38 = 36 + 2 = 6*6 + 2$ etc.

STOP! THINK! Don't let your mind wander here. When you understand this, it will seem incredibly obvious. Say it out loud:

> *"If the REMAINDER is <u>2</u> when you divide by 6, then the number we divided must be <u>2</u> more than a multiple of 6. So I'll pick ANY multiple of 6 and then I'll add 2."*

After all, if the number were an exact multiple of 6, then the remainder would have been zero. To make sure that there will be 2 left over, we add 2 to a multiple of 6. If we had wanted a different remainder, we would have started with a multiple of 6 and then added a different number. And if we were dividing by a different number, like say 9, then we would start with multiples of that number instead.

I'll write this as a general rule but it will sound very technical and intimidating:

> **To make up a number that has a certain remainder when divided by another number, called the divisor, start with any multiple of the divisor and then add the desired remainder.**

After you do a little practice, I think you will find that this is not a difficult trick. But how does it appear on the SAT? The next few examples will show you how and also give you a chance to practice.

We'll start with a grid-in:

If *X* is divided by 11, the remainder is 3. If *X* is a positive, even integer less than 50, find the sum of all possible values of *X*.

We want remainders of 3, so each of the possible numbers must be 3 more than a multiple of 11.

Examples could be 11+3=14, 22+3=25, 33+3=36, 44+3=47, 55+3=58...oh, wait, that last one is too big. And, as long as we are being careful, we should notice that the problem called for EVEN numbers, so we can't use 25 or 47. So that leaves us 14 and 36 as the only possible values for X. The problem asked for their sum, so: 14 + 36 = 50.

A Very Brief Psychological Digression:

Please notice that the last problem has a phrase that intimidates many test takers: "all possible values". Across the nation, students quake at those words. "Oh, man! I have to find EVERY possible value. This is going to be a nightmare." And then, of course, it turns out that it is not so bad. And the students who just stay calm and play with the problem find out that in this case "all possible" means "both". Sometimes it will be more than two, but it can't be so many that the problem takes more than a minute or two. And you are not in a hurry.

End of Digression.   On to the next example…

When n is divided by 7, the remainder is 3. When m is divided by 7, the remainder is 2.
What is the remainder when $m \times n + 1$ is divided by 7?

a) 0   **b) 1**   **c) 2**   **d) 3**   **e) 5**

This time, you are going to solve it.

First make up a POSSIBLE number for n:

(Remember, it has to be 3 more than a multiple of 7)

And now make up a number for m:

(This time, it's 2 more than a multiple of 7)

Now, find $m \times n + 1$:

OK, we are almost done. You just need to divide that last number by 7 and use the remainder finding trick...go do it and see what happens.

Did you get a little surprise? If you did this right, you found that there was NO remainder.
So the answer is choice 'a'. Score another victory for the method of making up numbers that fit the problem. And turn the page to find more practice.

Problem Set # 5: Remainder Problems

1. In a given year, New Year's Day falls on a Thursday. That year, Flag Day is the 165th day of the year. What day of the week will Flag Day be that year?

a) Sunday   b) Monday   c) Tuesday   d) Wednesday   e) Thursday

2. When k is divided by 8, the remainder is 2. Which of the following must be divisible by 8?

a) $2k$
b) $2k - 2$
c) $2k + 2$
d) $2k + 4$
e) $k/2 + 3$

3. When j and k are divided by 5, in either case, the remainder is 4. Which of the following must be divisible by 5?

a) $j - k$ b) $j + k$ c) $j \times k$ d) $j + k - 4$ e) $j - k + 4$

4. A coach lines up his football team, preparing to make 6 squads. He does this by "counting off" – going through the line, assigning players the numbers 1 through 6 repeatedly until every player has a number. If the last player gets assigned the number 3, which of the following could be the number of players in the line?

a) 18   b) 38   c) 42   d) 45   e) 48

5. (A Grid-in) Z is a positive integer which is divisible by both 3 and 5. When Z is divided by 7, the remainder is 4. What is the smallest possible value of Z?

6. (A Grid-in) At 2 pm, a TV station began playing 100 continuous hours of Simpsons reruns. What time did the reruns come to an end?

Set #5: Answer Key

1. The days of the week repeat in a pattern of 7. So we divide 165 by 7 and get 23.571428…Then, we drop the decimal and re-multiply: 23x7=161 which is 4 less than 165. So now we know the remainder is 4. (You can do long division if you prefer.) If the year began on a Thursday, then 4 days into the pattern is Thursday, Friday, Saturday, **Sunday**!
ANSWER: a

2. This looks like a Back Door problem. First we make up a number that fits. It has to be 2 more than a multiple of 8. I could use 10, 18, 82…but I'm feeling lazy, so I use 10. Then, I substitute k=10 into the answer choices, looking for a multiple of 8. And OH NO—d and e both give multiples of 8. So now I choose a new k value, say 18. Recheck d and e. This time, only d still works.
ANSWER: d

3. Another back door problem. Both j and k must be 4 more than a multiple of 5. I'll use j=24, k=14. Then, check each answer to see which is divisible by 5. This time, only a) works: j – k =24 – 14 = 10, and 10 is divisble by 5.
ANSWER: a

4. This is a pattern problem. There are 6 numbers in the pattern. And the coach ends up with 3 left over. So 3 must be the remainder when the number of players is divided by 6. You can check each number either by long division or by the calculator trick. Or, you can look for a number that you recognize as being 3 more than a multiple of 6…such as 45 which is 3 more than 42 which is 7x6.
ANSWER: d

5. Play around, looking for numbers that are divisible by 3 and 5. The smallest such number is 15. But 15 divided by 7 has remainder 1. (15 is 1 more than 14 which is a multiple of 7.) The next number that works is 30. But 30 divided by 7 has remainder 2. (30 is 3 more than 28.) Then 45…but 45 divided by 7 has remainder 3. (45 is 3 more than 42.) Do you get the feeling that the next one must be the one? 60 divided by 7 does have remainder 4. So we have our answer.
ANSWER: 60

6. The pattern here is the 12-hour pattern of clocks. 100 divided by 12 has remainder 4, so in 100 hours, the clock will read 4 hours later than 2:00 pm , which is… **6:00 pm**

Mean, Median and Mode

Somewhere, some time, some teacher taught you these terms. But it may have been three or four years ago. So I am going to review them for you. **Then, when you know these three definitions, be very aggressive about answering questions about them on the SAT.** They are usually easier than their placement in the section would lead you to believe, IF you know the definitions.[*] So here they are:

1. "MEAN"…also called "arithmetic mean"…also called "average":

The mean is what you get when you add up all the numbers you are given and then divide by how many there are. If you have ever calculated your test average in school, then you know how to do this. For example, if you have taken 5 tests and scored 90, 80, 95, 74 and 82, then your average score is $(90 + 80 + 82 + 74 + 95)/5 = 84.2$ That's all there is to it. But there are a few tricks worth knowing, which I will show you later in this section.

2. "MEDIAN"

The median is the middle number of the bunch, WHEN THE NUMBERS ARE WRITTEN IN ORDER (increasing or decreasing – it doesn't matter which). For example, if you need to find the median of the five test scores in the last example, the middle score was 95 but that was before we put the list in order. In order, it's 74, 80, 82, 90, 95 and the middle number is 82.

But what if there is no middle number?

By this question, students usually mean: what if there is an even number of numbers in the list? Then, there won't be just one number in the middle, but two. What do you do then?

I have two answers for you:

The Math Teacher Answer: You take the average of the two middle numbers. For example, if the numbers were 1, 3, 5, 10, 11, 100 then you would take the two middle numbers, 5 and 10, and then find the average of the two: $5 + 10 = 15$, $15 / 2 = 7.5$

The SAT Teacher Answer: In more than ten years, I have never seen an SAT problem that requires you to know how to do this. When they ask for a median, they give you an ODD number of numbers on the list. So don't worry about it.

3. "MODE"

The mode is the number that appears most often on the list. For example, if over a series of games, a baseball team scores 1, 0, 1, 1, 3, 4, 6, 2, 1, 4, and then 5 runs. What number appears the most? Obviously (I hope) the mode is 1.

---

[*] Why is this so? I believe that it is because the process of pre-screening questions does not reveal to ETS the reason WHY students get a question wrong. Some problems are hard because they are hard, and others are hard because you don't know the vocabulary. So if you DO know the vocabulary, you will think that the problem is easy. Of course, if you do NOT know the vocabulary, you have no chance.

Is there always a mode? Is there always only 1 mode?

Do you want the math teacher answer or the SAT teacher answer? I'll give you both. It's "No, no and don't worry about it." Here's why:

<u>No</u>, there is not always a mode. Consider, for example, the numbers 1,2,3,4,5,6. There is no mode.

<u>No</u>, there is not always just one mode. Consider, this time: 1,2,2,3,4,4,5,6. There are TWO modes, 2 and 4. (If you want to sound impressive, you say that the set is bi-modal.)

<u>Don't worry about it</u> because, as with medians, when they ask you for a mode, there will be one and only one for you to find.

Once you know all three definitions, you will find that many of these problems are straightforward. But there are a few wrinkles to watch out for. I'll illustrate them with examples.

1. Finding the median when the numbers are presented in chart form:

> **Lauren takes a survey of the students in her class to see how many children are in each of their families. She puts the results of her survey in a chart.**

Number of children in the family	Number of students with that number of children in their family
1	7
2	10
3	9
4	4
5	2
6	0
7	1

> **For example, 2 of the students in her class come from families with 5 children.**

> **What is the median number of children in the families of these students?**

> **a) 2   b) 3   c) 3   d) 4   e) 5**

The most commonly chosen WRONG answer is d) 4. People pick 4 because it is the middle number on the list of possible number of children. But that doesn't take into account HOW MANY times each number appears. If you listed the numbers of children in each family, taking into account how many times each number appears, you'd need seven 1's, ten 2's, etc...

Here's what your list should look like:

1, 1, 1, 1, 1, 1, 1, 2, 2, 2, 2, 2, 2, 2, 2, 2, 2, 3, 3, 3, 3, 3, 3, 3, 3, 3, 4,4, 4, 4, 5, 5, 7

Now, it's easy to find the middle number: the median is 2.

2. How will changing the data change the median? Or will it?

Try this question:

Dave took five history tests, steadily improving as he earned: 68, 70, 80, 82 and 85. Then, his teacher rescored his last two tests to give him extra credit for a project, raising each grade by 10 points. By how much did the median increase?

a) 0   b) 4   c) 5   d) 10   e) 20

Most people who get this wrong either misread the question or they calculate averages instead of medians. If you remember to find the medians, it is not that hard, especially because the numbers are already in order. Of 68, 70, 80, 82 and 85, I hope it's obvious that the middle number is 80.

Then, after the extra credit is awarded, the numbers are now 68, 70, 80, 92 and 95. But look! The median is STILL 80. It did not change, because…

When you have a set of numbers, if you increase some of the numbers that were already higher than the median, the median does not change.

So the sets {3,4,5}, {3,4,10} and {3,4,1000000} all have the same median. And the same is true if you decrease numbers that were already below the median.[*]

We'll get to some practice problems soon. But there is one more twist you need to see first. If we are going to continue to avoid algebra at every turn, you need to see how to make up numbers when it's a little trickier.

---

[*] In the world of descriptive statistics, this is what makes the median a more useful measure than the mean. It is less sensitive to extreme variations in outlying data points.

"Average" Problems the Easy Way – Making up Numbers (again!)

I'm not talking about a problem that is average in difficulty. I am taking about a problem that involves the average of a bunch of numbers. Some people say you should use algebra for these problems because making up numbers is too difficult. But I am not one of those people. It is NOT too hard to make up numbers that have a certain average. You just have to follow two easy rules:

Rule #1: Start with the laziest possible numbers.

Rule #2: Adjust those lazy numbers until they fit EVERYTHING the problem says.

So let's begin by learning how to be lazy. Here is a warm-up exercise:

Tell me three numbers that have an average (arithmetic mean) of 14.

(Hint: I want the absolute LAZIEST numbers you can think of.)

Do NOT read any further until you have written your three numbers in the boxes.

Do you want to know if your numbers are correct? You don't need to ask me—just add them up and then divide by three. If you get 14 as the average, then your numbers are correct. If not, then you definitely need to learn a trick. And even if you got it right, are your numbers the laziest numbers possible? I'm about to tell you my numbers, so if you have not yet made up your own, this is really your last chance…. OK, here goes:

My numbers were 14, 14 and 14. Isn't that lazy? That's what I always do: I begin making up numbers by making all of the numbers the same is the average. Then, I adjust them to fit the problem better. What do I mean? Well, try these two:

Find three <u>different</u> numbers that have an average of 14:

Find three numbers that have an average of 14, where two of the numbers are the same and one is different:

If you are stuck, let me help. Here's the first one:

We start with the lazy numbers: 14   14   14

But the problem said they all have to be different, so we are going to have to adjust these numbers – without changing the average! So, the rule about adjusting the numbers is:

To keep the average the same, however much you increase one of the numbers, you must decrease one of the others by the same amount.

Think of it as piles of rocks. Then, if you move the rocks from pile to pile, the number of rocks in each pile changes but the average stays the same.

So let's go back to the piles with 14 rocks in each one, and we'll move one rock from the first pile to the last pile. Now are numbers are:

                    13   14   15   which are all different and still average 14.

And of course, we could have moved more than 1 rock and it didn't matter which pile we moved it to, but why not do it the easiest way we can think of.

For the second problem, again we start with 14, 14 and 14. Now we want two of the same and one different. There are a lot of ways to do this. One way is to take two rocks off the first pile and put one of them on each of the other two piles. So we end up with 12, 15 and 15. Two the same, one not. Add 'em up, divide by three and sure enough, you get 14. How about that.

Here are two more for you to try. The solutions are on the next page.

A baseball team averages 5 runs scored per game over a span of 6 games. The team scored one run in the first game, two runs in the second game, three runs in the third game and four runs in the fourth game. What is the average of the runs they scored in games five and six?

After four tests, Dylan has an average of 85. His lowest score was an 82 and all of his test scores were different whole numbers. What is the highest he could have scored on any one test?

We'll start with the baseball team. They averaged 5 runs per game for six games. So let's make them all 5's:

> 5   5   5   5   5   5

(We know that this isn't going to be right. But this is how we start.)

The first game's score was only 1 run. So we'll change the 5 to a 1. But if we take 4 rocks off that pile, we have to add them to some other pile. I'm going to add them to the last pile. So now, we have:

> 1   5   5   5   5   9

Then, we change the second game score to a 2. That's a decrease of 3. So we add 3 somewhere else…it doesn't matter where. Why not the last pile again? Ok…

> 1   2   5   5   5   12

Then…

> 1   2   3   5   5   14

And…

> 1   2   3   4   5   15

These numbers fit the question. They still have an average of 5 – check for yourself if you don't believe me. And now, the rest of the problem is easy – you just have to find the average of the last two games: 5 + 15 =20, 20/2 = 10. That's it!

And now it's Dylan's turn. He had an 85-test average after four tests. So let's say:

85   85   85   85

But one of them was an 82…so we'll move three rocks from one pile to another:

82   85   85   88

So is 88 the highest he could have scored? No, we're not done. We can move more rocks! Since 82 is the lowest and they all have to be different, we can make one 83 and another 84…but then we'll have to increase the 88, first by 2 and then by 1 more…

82   83   84   91

So 91 is his highest possible score. I bet he practiced. Now it's your turn.

Practice Set # 6: Mean, Median and Mode

Questions 1 – 3 refer to the following information:

The integers from 2 through 8 are each raised to the 4th power, with the <u>units digit</u> of the resulting number recorded in the second column of the table shown.

2	
3	
4	
5	
6	
7	
8	

1. The mean of the entries in the second column is approximately:

    a) 4.2   b) 4.4   c) 5.0   d) 20.0   e) 625.0

2. The mode of the entries in the second column is:

    a) 1   b) 2   c) 4   d) 5   e) 6

3. When the median of the first column is subtracted from the median of the second column, the result is:

    a) –2   b) –1   c) 0   d) 1   e) 2

4. (A Grid-in) Kyle is looking at a calendar for the month of October, which has 31 days, noticing which of the numbers on the calendar are prime. Of the "prime" days in October, which is the median?

5. Going into the last game of the basketball season, Sam was averaging 18 points per game. He scored 32 points in the last game, bringing his scoring average up to exactly 20 points per game. How many games did he play all together (including the last one)?

    a) 5   b) 7   c) 8   d) 14   e) 16

6. If the average of x, x and y is 6 more than y, then $y = \ldots$

    a) $x - 9$
    b) $2x - 6$
    c) $6 - 2x$
    d) $x/2 - 9$
    e) $3 - x$

Set #6: Answer Key

Before you can answer questions 1 – 3, you have to complete the chart. You do this by following the directions: you take each entry, raise it to the fourth power and then write the units digit (that's the ONES digit) in the chart. For example, $2^4=1\underline{6}$ so we put a 6 in the chart. The completed chart looks like this:

Now you are ready to answer the questions:

2	6
3	1
4	6
5	5
6	6
7	1
8	6

1. To find the mean, add them up and divide:
$(6+1+6+5+6+1+6)=31$, $31/7=4.428...$and they did use the word "approximately" which tells you that you may have to round off your answer.
ANSWER: b

2. The mode is just the number appearing most on the list: clearly (I hope) it's 6.
ANSWER: e

3. The median in the first column is the middle number, 5, because they are already in order.
The second column must be put in order: 1, 1, 5, 6, 6, 6, 6. Then, the middle number is 6. So we subtract $6 – 5 =1$.
ANSWER: d

4. We start by listing the prime numbers, up to and including 31. That would be: 2, 3, 5, 7, 11, 13, 17, 19, 23, 29, 31. Then, we find the middle number, 13, and we're done.
ANSWER: 13

5. We are going to use trial and error, along with the trick of making all the numbers the same.
If 'a' is the answer, then he played in 5 games and averaged 18 per game until he scored 32 in the last game. So his scores could have been: 18, 18, 18, 18, 32. So if we add these up and divide by 5, we'll have his average: $(18+18+18+18+32)/5=20.8$ which is <u>close</u> to 20, but not exactly right. And they didn't say anything about "approximately" here. So let's try 'b'.
If he played 7 games, averaging 18 until the 32 in the last game, his scores could have been: 18, 18, 18, 18, 18, 18, 32. And if we average those numbers, we get $(18+18+18+18+18+18+32)/6=20$ which is just what we were looking for.
ANSWER: b

6. It's a Back Door problem, but making up the numbers is a little tricky. As always, I start with all of the numbers the same. So, for x, x and y I'll say: 20, 20 and 20. But now the average is not 6 more than y. I need to make y less by 6, without changing the average. Oh, I know! I'll move rocks off the y pile and on to the x piles. If I take 6 away from y, it will be 14. Put 3 each on the two x-piles. Now the numbers are 23, 23 and 14. The average is still 20, and y is 6 less than that.

Now what do they want to know? Just the value of y. Well, I know that: $y=14$.

Finally, plug $x=23$ into each answer choice. The only matching choice is a) $x-9 = 23 – 9 = 14$.
ANSWER: a

Percents and Percent Changes

There will definitely be at least one or two questions on your SAT that require some percent-related skills. I will begin with the most fundamental of the skills and then move on from there.

Percent Skill #1: Finding a given percent of a given number
(This is not something that the SAT will ask you. They will ask you a more complicated question that requires this skill as one step.)

For example, what is 35% of 240?

The FASTEST way to do this is to let your calculator help you. You need to know two things:

1. Your calculator has a "%" button.
2. "Of" means "times" (but not always – let's just use this as a middle school rule)

So you press: **35 % × 240 ENTER** and your calculator says: **84**

(If you knew that 35% is the same is as 0.35, you could do it that way too.)

Percent Skill #2: Deciding if an answer is reasonable

Here are some guidelines to help to get a feel for how big a percent answer should be.

1. 100% is all of the number. 200% is twice the number. 300% is three times the number.

2. 50% is half, 25% is a quarter, $33^1/_3$% is one third

3. 10% is one tenth. This one is easy to do in your head. You move the decimal one place.

   For example, 10% of 625 is 62.5

Now, you might be thinking: "Why should I bother knowing this when I have a calculator?" Well, even when you use a calculator, you should look at the answer and think about whether it makes sense. You may have pressed a wrong button or made some other little mistake. So you want to get in the habit of looking at the answers with a critical eye.

For example, we used a calculator to find that 35% of 240 is 84. Could that be right? Well, 35% is a little more than a third, and a third of 240 is 80. So this looks ok.

Also, when you know how to come up with a ballpark estimate, you can rule out multiple-choice answers that are not even close.

Percent Skill #3: When the percent is not what you are looking for...

The best way for me to explain is with an example:

70 is 140% of what number?

I have two ways for you to approach problems like this.

Method #1 -- Trial and Error (Longer, but less algebra)

If the only percent skill you have is the first one, where you find a given percent of a given number, then this is the method for you. If there are answer choices, you use them as your guesses. But if there are no answer choices, you take a guess. (See page _____)

So let's guess. I'll guess 120.

Is 70 140% of 120? Use your calculator...**140% × 120 = 168, which is not 70!**

In fact, 120 was NOT a good guess. Let's think about it: 140% is more than the whole amount. So the number we are looking for is LESS than 70. Let's try 40.

140% × 40 = 56...which is too small. So we'll try something bigger, say 60...
140% × 60 = 84...which is too big. Let's try 50.
140% × 50 = 70!!!

Method #2 – "Is" over "of" = % over 100 (Uses algebra, but it's faster)

I'm talking about using the proportion: $\dfrac{"is"}{"of"} = \dfrac{\%}{100}$

I know that many schools teach this method. It's pretty straightforward. In the wording of the problem, they will tell you two of the three numbers—the "is", the "of", and the %. Whichever one they do NOT tell you, you call 'x'. Then, you write the proportion, cross-multiply and then divide. Let's look at that last one again.

70 is 140% of what number?

The "is" is 70. The % is 140. We don't know the "of" so we call it 'x'.

So the proportion is: $\dfrac{70}{x} = \dfrac{140}{100}$

Cross-multiply: $7000 = 140x$

Divide (both sides, by 140): $50 = x$

This is one algebraic procedure that is worth knowing.

Percent Skill #4: Percent Increases and Decreases

Ok, this skill is really TWO skills and then one trick. The two skills are:

1. Given the original amount and the new amount, find the size of the percent change.

2. Given an original amount and the size of the percent change, find the new amount.

So let's take a look, one at a time. (Is there any other way?)

Last year, Sharon earned $8.00 per hour at the grocery store. This year, she earns $9.60 per hour at the video store. What is the percent increase in her hourly pay?

The easiest way to do this is to memorize the following rule:

$$Percent\ change = \frac{change}{starting} \times 100$$

So in this case, the change was $9.60 - $8.00 = $1.60 and the starting amount was $8.00 so…

$$Percent\ change = \frac{change}{start} \times 100 = \frac{1.6}{8} \times 100 = 20\%$$

So if you know the change and the starting amount, you are in business. Next:

In the beginning of the track season, Frank ran 100 meters in 11.2 seconds. By the end of the season, he had reduced his time by 5%. What was the new time?

You could do this by using the same rule as last time, but then you would need to do a little algebra. But finding new values after percent increases or decreases is NOT an algebra problem. All it takes is arithmetic (which you do with your calculator).

We start by finding the given percent of the starting value. In this case, it's 5% of 11.2 which, as we saw in Percent Skill #1 is just:

5 % x 11.2 = 0.56

Then, you either increase or decrease the starting value by the number you have just found. This time, it was a reduction, so we subtract:

11.2 − 0.56 = 10.64

so the new time is 10.64 seconds.

And now, one of the SAT's favorite traps…

Multiple Percent Changes in succession:

If a problem has some value that experiences some percent change, followed by ANOTHER percent change (and maybe even another one after that), the important thing to know is that the NEW percent change is based on the NEW starting amount and NOT on the original starting amount. A few examples should help explain what I mean:

Jack earned \$120 mowing lawns when he was a freshman. Then, for each of the following years, he earned 10% more than in the previous year. What did he earn in his senior (4th) year?

The first step is to find 10% of \$120. You can use your calculator, or in this case, since 10% is one that you have memorized (right?!?), you can just move the decimal place. Either way, you should find that 10% of 120 is 12. But now, we better be careful…here comes the trap.

Wrong Answer:

So if it went up by 10% three times, and 10% is \$12, then the total increase is \$36. So he earned \$120 +\$36 = \$156 in his senior year.

Why it's wrong:

\$12 is only 10% of the FIRST year's earnings. Each year, as he earns more money, 10% becomes a bigger number too.

So what do you do?

You have to figure out the increase each year, one at a time, like this:

10% of \$120 is \$12. \$120 + \$12 = \$132, so \$132 is the second year earnings.

Then, 10% of \$132 is \$13.20 and \$132 + \$13.20 = \$145.20, which is the third year earnings.

And finally, 10% of \$145.20 is \$14.52 and \$145.20 + \$14.52 is \$159.72, the senior year earnings and our answer to the question.

ACTUAL MATH: MIDDLE SCHOOL

ALTERNATE METHOD FOR PERCENT CHANGES:

A quick way to increase a number by 10% is to multiply it by 1.1 – so this time, we could have taken the original number, $120, and multiplied it by 1.1 three times. Try it and see! And this trick works for other percent changes, too. I've put it all into the chart below. It's a quick trick, if you can keep it straight, but if you can't, then just stick to the method I've already shown you. It takes a little longer, but it works too.

Quick Way to do Percent Changes

For a 10%...	INCREASE:	Multiply by 1.1
	DECREASE:	Multiply by .9
For a 20%...	INCREASE:	Multiply by 1.2
	DECREASE:	Multiply by .8
For a 30%...	INCREASE:	Multiply by 1.3
	DECREASE:	Multiply by .7
For a 40%...	INCREASE:	Multiply by 1.4
	DECREASE:	Multiply by .6
And in general,		
For a N%...	INCREASE:	Multiply by $(1 + N/100)$
	DECREASE:	Multiply by $(1 - N/100)$

This method is especially helpful in a problem like the last one, with multiple percent changes. Let's try another:

A bicycle originally cost $200. The price is decreased by 30% but then the price was increased by 40%. Compared to the original price, the final price was:

a) $4 more   b) $4 less   c) $10 more   d) $20 more   e) $20 less

89

So we start with $200. Use either of the two methods that I have shown you to decrease this by 30% (find 30% and subtract it from 200 OR multiply 200 by .7) – do this right now…

…and then check to see if you are doing it right so far.[*] Then take that answer and increase it by 40% (find 40% of that answer and add it OR multiply by 1.4)…

and you are ready to compare[†]. The new price is $4 less than the original price. So the answer is b) $4 less.

---

[*] You should have $140
[†] Now you should have $196

Practice Set # 7: Percent Problems

1. Ben works at a store where a shirt has a regular price of $60. Its price is reduced by 25% for a sale. Then, Ben uses his employee discount to purchase the shirt for $30. What percent is the employee discount?

a) 15% b) 25% c) $33^{1}/3$% d) 50 % e) $66^{2}/3$%

2. 25% of 50 is 50% of what number?

a) 6.25 b) 12.5 c) 25 d) 100 e) 150

3. (A Grid-In) There are 15 boys and 25 girls on Mrs. Quigley's school bus. If 20% of the boys bring their lunch and 30% of all of the students bring their lunch, how many girls bring their lunch to school?

4. Starting from a price of $400, two successive increases of n% increased the price to $900. What is the value of n?

a) 50 b) 62.5 c) 125 d) 250 e) 500

5. The population of Redwood is 300 people. If the population increases by 15% each year for a number of years in a row, approximately how many years will it take for the population to double?

a) 5 b) 6 c) 7 d) 15 e) 40

6. What percentage of a complete revolution does the minute hand of a clock complete between 1:15pm and 1:24pm on the same day?

a) 9% b) 10% c) 15% d) 18% e) 40%

Set #7: Answer Key

1. Because the $60 price is reduced by 25%, we should find 25% of 60 and then subtract. We can use a calculator, but since 25% is 1/4 , we don't need one. It's $15. So the reduced price is 60 –15 = $45. But Ben only pays $30, so his employee discount saved him an additional $15. But that is NOT another 25%. This time, it was 15 out of 45 which is 1/3 or $33^1/3$%.
ANSWER: c

2. 25% of 50 is 12.5. You can find this by multiplying 25%x50 or, again, by recognizing that 25% is the same as ¼. Either way, you get 12.5, so now you have to figure out what number is it that 12.5 is 50% of? And since 50% is also ½, the answer is 25—12.5 is half of 25.
ANSWER: c

3. Of the 15 boys, if 20% bring lunch, that makes 20% of 15, which is 3. And of the 40 kids altogether, 30% bring their lunch. That's 30% of 40, which is 12. So if 12 kids overall bring lunch, and 3 boys bring lunch, then 9 girls must also bring their lunch to school.
ANSWER: 9

4. Best way is trial and error. Starting with 'a': If we increase 400 by 50%, that will be 400 + 200 (because 200 is 50% of 400) which gives us 600. Then, 50% of 600 is 300 and 600 + 300 = 900 – so we are done!
ANSWER: a

5.Start with 300. Find 15% of 300 and add it on. Now, you should have 345. Find 15% of that, and add it on. Now, you are at 396.75. Keep repeating the process, and see when you reach 600. Or, if you want to use the quicker way, start with 300. Keep multiplying what you have by 1.15. The 5th time you do it, you'll land on 603.4.
ANSWER: a

6. From 1:15pm to 1:24pm is an interval of 9 minutes. But that does NOT make 'a' the right answer. The question asks, "what percent of a <u>complete revolution</u>", and a complete revolution of the minute hand is 60 minutes. I can use my calculator now, but as always, I'm feeling lazy...so let's think: 10% of 60 would be 6 minutes. 20% would be twice that, or 12 minutes. The 9 minutes must be midway between 10% and 20%...so I know the answer is c: 15%. But, if you are not feeling confident about that, go ahead and check. Calculate 15% of 60. You won't be surprised.
ANSWER: c

Ratios and Proportions

A proportion is a statement that two ratios are equal…oh, I'm sorry. Did I put you to sleep? Algebra will do that sometimes. And yet, though I hate to admit it, in this case what you learned in algebra class is actually the easiest way. And since ratio problems appear on most SAT's, we'd better make sure you can do them.

The trick is to see that all ratio problems are the same. You have these two quantities. They are changing. So they had old values and they now have new values. But the ratios stay the same. So you have to set up that same proportion every time:

$$\frac{Thing1}{Thing2} = \frac{Other1}{Other2}$$

Now, when you read the problem, you are going to find that they tell you THREE out of the four values that go in this ratio. And it's your job to find the FOURTH one. So you fill in the numbers that you know and you call the one you don't know 'x'. At that point, your proportion looks like this:

$$\frac{number}{number} = \frac{number}{x}$$ (But the x can be in any one of the four positions in the proportion).

And then you cross-multiply and divide…and you are done!

Of course, I am going to show you a few examples. First, review the following list of commonly encountered ratio situations. These will probably be familiar to you from algebra class. I've seen each of them on the SAT.

When Thing 1 is Proportional to Thing 2:

1. Recipes…the amount of an ingredient is proportional to the number of servings

2. Map Scales…the distance on the map is proportional to the distance in the world
   This also applies to scale drawings (such as blueprints) as well.

3. Similar Triangles…corresponding sides are proportional
   The building height, building shadow problem is an example of this.
   And it applies to any "similar" geometric figures, not just triangles. (See page 107.)

4. Rate · Time = Distance…so distance traveled is proportional to the time spent,
   and distance traveled is also proportional to rate of travel.
   However, Rate and Time are NOT proportional.

Then, there are two traps to watch out for.

RATIO TRAP #1: Be Consistent! If your first ratio has "Thing 1" on top, you MUST also put the other "Thing 1" on top.

RATIO TRAP #2: The UNITS have to be the same!

Example:

A recipe that makes 2 dozen cookies requires 1½ cups of sugar. To make 60 cookies, using the same recipe, how much sugar would be required?

a) 1/20 cup   b) 3 cups   c) 3¾ cups   d) 12 cups   e) 45 cups

Ok, first thing is that the units have to be the same. So we can't be talking about "dozens" of cookies in one ratio, and individual cookies in the other. So we'll replace the "2 dozen" with "24". (Or, we could replace the "60 cookies" with "5 dozen" if we thought of it.)

Then, we have to pick thing 1 and thing 2 so we can write the proportion. It does not matter which one you put on top. ALL THAT MATTERS IS THAT YOU ARE CONSISTENT! I'm going to put cookies on top and sugar on bottom:

$$\frac{24 \text{ cookies}}{1\frac{1}{2} \text{ cups}} = \frac{60 \text{ cookies}}{x \text{ cups}}$$

Then, we cross multiply…

$$24x = 60 \times 1\frac{1}{2} \text{ or } 24x = 90$$

And then divide…

$$x = 90/24 = 3\frac{3}{4}…\textit{There! Was that so hard?}$$

Well, no. It really is not that difficult a procedure as algebra goes. That's why I recommend it. But that doesn't mean that you HAVE to use algebra. Here's another way you could approach this problem:

Well, let' see. First of all, 60 cookies is more than 24 cookies. Duh. So we'll need more sugar. In fact, we'll need more than twice has much sugar (60 is more that double 24) but not quite three times as much sugar (60 is less than triple 24). So I need something that is more than 1½ doubled, which is 3, and less than 1 ½ tripled…the only answer that fits is choice 'c'.

So once again, the kid who PLAYS avoids algebra and gets the answer. But, to be fair, he was lucky that this one was multiple-choice.

Practice Set #8: Ratio Problems

1. (Grid-In) Michael lives 2.5 miles away from the train station. On his map, the train station is 1.5 inches away from his house, and the City Zoo is 2.4 inches away from his house. How far away from the City Zoo does Michael live?

2. (Grid-In) Caitlin competed in a swim-a-thon to raise money for charity. She found people who sponsored her, agreeing to donate money for every lap that she swam. She managed to swim 140 laps, raising $175. But she wanted to raise $200, so how many <u>additional</u> laps did she need to swim?

3. If the ratio of $2x$ to $3y$ is equal to the ratio of x to $2z$, then the ratio of y to z is:

    a) 2/3   b) 3/2   c) ¾   d) 4/3   e) 2/1

4. Joseph runs 50 yards in 12 seconds. At that speed, how many <u>feet</u> can he run in 30 seconds?

    a) 37   b) 125   c) 375   d) 750   e) 1500

5. (A grid-in) A jar contains red candies and blue candies. If 2/5th of the candies in the jar are red, find the ratio of blue candies to red candies.

6 Mary and Frank each have their own maps of their town. On Mary's map, the school and the zoo are 4 inches apart. On Frank's map, the school and the mall are 6 inches apart. From this information, we can conclude:

a) The school and zoo are closer to each other than the school and the mall are.
b) The school and the zoo are further apart than the school and the mall are.
c) Mary's map is drawn to a smaller scale than Frank's.
d) Frank's map is drawn to a smaller scale than Mary's.
e) None of the above

Set #8: Answer Key

1. A classic ratio problem: $\dfrac{2.5miles}{1.5inches} = \dfrac{x}{2.4inches}$ and then you cross-multiply and divide. You get: $1.5x = 6$, so $x = 4$ miles.
ANSWER: 4

2. This time, the ratio is: $\dfrac{140}{\$175} = \dfrac{x}{\$200}$, but then, after you cross-multiply and divide to get $x= 160$ laps, you have to remember what the question asked: how many <u>additional</u> laps? So we subtract $160 - 140 = 20$ more laps.
ANSWER: 20

3. Let's just make up numbers that fit and then see what happens. Suppose x = 10 and y = 20. Then the ratio of 2x to 3y is 20 to 60 which is the same as 1 to 3. Now, if x to 2z has that same ratio, and x = 10, then 2z has to be 30, so z has to be 15. (But wait! How did I get started? Where did x = 10 and y = 20 come from? I just MADE THEM UP! You can start with different numbers. You can start in a different order. Just jump in and play.) So now we have possible numbers for x, y and z. With our numbers, the ratio of y to z is 20 to 15, and 20/15 reduces to 4/3, which is the answer.
ANSWER: d

4. This is a classic ratio—but watch the units: $\dfrac{50yds}{12\sec} = \dfrac{x}{30\sec}$ is the setup. But after you cross-multiply and divide, you now have 125 <u>yards</u>. Which is, of course, 375 <u>feet</u>.
ANSWER: c

5. Let's make up numbers: How about 100 candies, of which two fifths are red. That would be 40 red candies (100x 2/5 or $100 \div 5 = 20$ and then 20 x 2 = 40. Then that makes 60 candies that are blue. So the ratio of blue to red is 60/40 which reduces to…**ANSWER: 3/2 or 1.5**

6. Well, let's think. These two people are looking at DIFFERENT MAPS! And different maps sometimes have DIFFERENT SCALES! So there is NO WAY to determine which distance is actually greater.
ANSWER: e

Round 2 – Geometry

This is one of those good news/bad news situations. Bad news first: You DO need to know some geometry. It's the school math topic that you cannot avoid on the SAT. Oh, well.

Now the good news: you don't need to know a LOT of geometry. There are many topics in a typical high school geometry course that never make it onto the SAT. The topics that do appear can be reviewed pretty quickly by reading this section.

And more good news: the SAT likes to combine geometry problems with algebra. This IS good news because you can continue to use all of the algebra-avoiding tricks you have learned so far.

The topics in this section are:

> All About Angles
>
> Four Useful (Though Kind of Dull) Triangle Facts
>
> Pythagorean Theorem (including Special Right Triangles)
>
> Areas and especially Areas of Shaded Regions

About Scale Drawings:

The diagrams on the SAT are drawn to scale, unless they say otherwise. And sometimes, they do just that: at the bottom of the picture, it will say "Figure not drawn to scale". Now why would they do that? Here are two possible reasons:

1. They want to see if you will be fooled into making judgments based on appearances.
2. The problem would be too easy if the diagram were drawn to scale.

In other words, once again, they are out to get you. You can avoid this kind of trap by re-drawing the diagram for yourself, as neatly as you can. In fact, taking the time to draw neat diagrams is helpful in a number of different situations, as you will see.

All About Angles

I have a collection of angle facts for you to review. At the end of the collection, I will show you some sample questions and give you some practice to do. But you have to wait until the end of the collection because the SAT rarely asks angle questions that are based on a <u>single</u> geometric fact. They blend two or three concepts into one question, so you need to know the whole set. Here goes…

1. A full circle forms a 360° angle. So, for example, the marked angle below is 340°.

2. A straight line makes an angle of 180°. So, for example, if we were trying to make up numbers for the diagram below, we could pick anything we want, as long as the x, the $3x$ and the y all add up to 180.

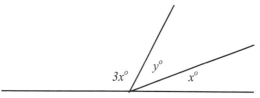

Say we picked $x = 35$. Then $3x = 105$. Together, that makes $35 + 105 = 140$. We need to get to 180, so we let $y = 40$, and we are all set.

3. "Vertical Angles" are equal. We are talking about the 2 pairs of angles that are formed when two lines intersect.

There are three easy rules to remember here:

The acute angles are equal to each other.
The obtuse angles are equal to each other.
An acute + an obtuse = 180°.

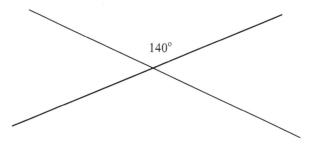

So if you know ONE of the angles, you know the other three. For example, you should be able to find the missing angles in the diagram above.

4. Parallel lines and transversals. In school, you learned a whole collection of vocabulary devoted to this subject: "alternate interior", "alternate exterior", "same-side interior", and so on. You don't need any of those terms on the SAT. The same rules we used for vertical angles also apply here:

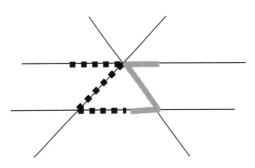

The acute angles are equal to each other.
The obtuse angles are equal to each other.
An acute + an obtuse = 180.

But there is one trick that the SAT uses to try to foil you: They put multiple lines on the same diagram. Then, there are more than one set of acute and obtuse angles. How can you tell which ones go together?

Draw a 'Z'. The angles formed will be equal.

Look at the diagram.
The different Z's are used
to highlight angles that are equal[*].

5. The angles of a triangle add up to 180.

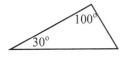

So in this case, the missing angle can be found by adding the two you know and then subtracting that total from 180.

6. The angles of a quadrilateral add up to 360 (because any quadrilateral can be cut by a diagonal into two triangles).

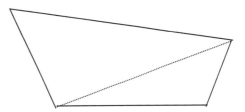

7. The angles of a pentagon add up to 540 (because any pentagon can be cut into three triangles by two diagonals).

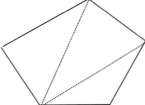

You may remember seeing a rule for a polygon with 'n' sides: the angles add up to (n-2)·180, but I've never seen a problem that needed this formula.

---

[*] There is a legitimate math reason that this trick works. The letter 'Z' is formed by making two parallel segments, connected by a transversal. Tracing a 'Z' onto a complicated diagram forces you to focus on ONE pair of parallel lines and the transversal that connects them.

8. The base angles of an isosceles triangle are equal.
   And this means that you only need one angle to find the other two.
   Look at the triangle on the right.
   We know that x must also be 75.
   And then, because the total must be 180,
   we can find the third angle:
   $75 + 75 = 150$. $180 - 150 = 30$.
   So $30°$ is the other missing angle, $y°$.

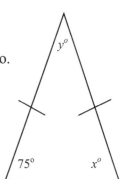

9. If all of the sides of a triangle are equal, then all three angles are equal.
   So they must be $60°$ each.

And that's it! That's all of the angle facts you need on the SAT. Of course, it wouldn't be the SAT if it were not evil. They must have a way of making life difficult for you. Actually, they have a number of ways...let's see some examples.

1. Multiple facts in a single question:

If AB = BC, and the marked angle is 310°, then what is the value of x?

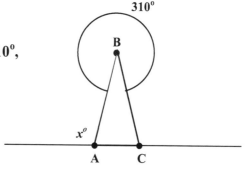

A) 50   B) 65   C) 115   D) 125   E) 155

Note the sequence of concepts that you need to apply:

1. Because the whole circle is $360°$, the vertex angle of the isosceles triangle is $360 - 310 = 50°$.
2. The triangle's angles add up to $180°$, so the base angles add up to $180 - 50 = 130°$.
3. The two base angles are equal so they are each $130/2 = 65°$.
4. The straight line is $180°$, so $x = 180 - 65 = 115°$.

     None of the individual steps are difficult. You just have to be on the lookout for problems that combine a variety of angle facts. More examples coming soon, but first let's look at another way they can twist these problems...

2. Algebra inside geometry problems

I love problems like this next one. They look SO hard, and then you apply the concepts we have just reviewed, along with the Back Door trick, and the problem becomes EASY!

In the figure shown, line AB is parallel to line CD. Which of the following expressions gives the value of *x* in terms of *y*?

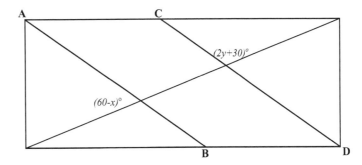

A) 2y - 90
B) 30 – 2y
C) y/2 + 30
D) 90 – 2y
E) 2y + 30

Now look at this thing. It has all the signals that tell you to use the back door trick: there are variables in the question, there are variables in the answer choices, and it even has the phrase "in terms of…". So we use the three-step procedure that lets us avoid algebra.

1. Make up numbers for x and y.

But, as I hope you remember, the numbers we choose must fit the problem. In this case, that means following the rules of geometry. Here's what I mean:

If we choose $x = 20$, then that angle is $60 – 20 = 40°$. Now the trick is to realize that what we have here are two parallel lines crossed by a transversal (it helps if you look at the diagram with your head tilted to the right). So we can figure out the other angles: the acute ones are $40°$ and the obtuse angles are $140°$. That means $2y + 30 = 140$. So $y = 55$.

These are NOT the only numbers that work. I chose $x = 20$ because it was the first thing I thought of. You could pick other values for *x*. Or you could start by making up a value for *y* first. You just have to find a pair of numbers that fit.

2. Use YOUR numbers to answer THEIR question.

Aha! This time, it's easy. They wanted to know the value of *x*. And we already know it. It's 20, just like we picked it.

3. Substitute YOUR numbers into THEIR answers, checking for answers that match yours.

A) 2y – 90.... 2˙55 – 90 = 20… yes
B) 30 – 2y … 30 - 2˙55 = -80… no
C) y/2 + 30 … 55/2 + 30 = 57.5 …no
D) 90 – 2y … 90 - 2˙55 = -20 … no (almost, but still no)
E) 2y + 30 … 2˙55 +30 = 140 … no.

And since 'A' is the only match, that's it.

Practice Set #9: All About Angles

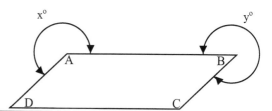

1. Given that ABCD is a parallelogram, and that x and y are the measures of the two marked angles, what is the sum of x and y?

a) 180   b) 2 70   c) 360   d) 540   e) 720

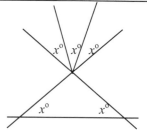

2. All five angles indicated in the diagram at right have equal measure, $x°$. What is the value of x?

a) 36   b) 45   c) 60   d) 72   e) 90

3. Which expression gives the value of y as shown in the diagram at right?

a) $2x - 180$
b) $180 - 2x$
c) $2a - 180$
d) $180 - 2a$
e) $2x + 180$

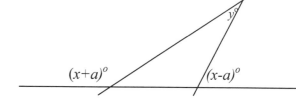

4. Lines ℓ and m are parallel. They are crossed by lines p and q. Line p is perpendicular to line ℓ. Lines p, q and m all intersect, forming the angles whose measures are indicated in the diagram. Determine the value of x.

a) 10   b) 15   c) 20   d) 25   e) 30

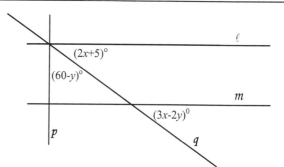

5. (A Grid-in) Find the average of the measures of the five marked angles, a, b, c, d and e.

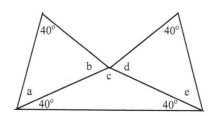

6. (A grid-in)

Given that $a + c = 200$, find $b + d$.

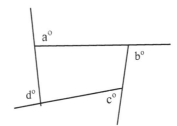

Set #9: Answer Key

1. To begin, we can make up possible angles for the parallelogram. We can use any numbers we want, as long as the acute angles are the same, the obtuse angles are the same and the acute + the obtuse = 180. (Why? Because a parallelogram consists of parallel lines connected by transversals.) So, for example, at A and B you could say....

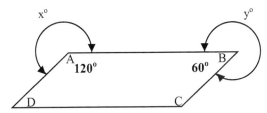

Then, because circles add up to 360°, we can find x and y: x = 360 – 120 = 240 and y = 360 – 60 = 300.
Finally, x + y = 540.
ANSWER: d

2. In this problem, the key is to notice that the 3 little angles on the top of the diagram form one big angle that is equal to the top angle in the triangle.

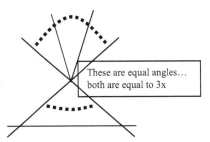

These are equal angles... both are equal to 3x

Then, the angles of the triangle add up to 5x, so **5x = 180**, which you can solve by dividing both sides by 5, or by trial and error with the answer choices. Either way, you get x = 36.
ANSWER: a

3. This is a Back Door problem. So we start by making up numbers that fit. For example:
If we choose x = 100 and a = 40 then the exterior angle on the left is 140 and the exterior angle on the right is 60.
Then, we can find the angles inside the triangle. On the left, it's 180 – 140 = 40. On the right, 180 – 60 = 120.
And if you have two of the angles of a triangle, then you can find the third...so y = 180 – (40 +120) = 20.

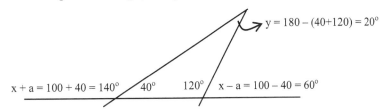

(Once again, note that when it is difficult to make up the numbers, the rest of the process is easy.)

Now, what do they ask for? Just the value of y. We know that: y = 20.

So we go to the answer choices, plug in our x and a values...and the only match is choice a) 2x – 180 = 200 – 180 = 20.

ANSWER: a

4. Those of you who like algebra can set up a system of two equations and two unknowns. Those of you who don't like algebra should go the answer choices and use trial and error…

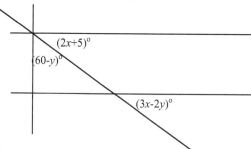

Could x = 10? If it did, then 2x+5 = 25.
But that's a right angle, so the rest would have to be 65, which would make y = -5.
Now, if x = 10 and y = -5, then 3x - 2y = 30 - -10 = 40. But that can't be right, because the lines are parallel, but 40 is not equal to 25. I guess x isn't 10.

Could x = 15? 2x + 5 = 35. 90 – 35 = 55 = 60 – y. So y = 5. And that makes 3x – 2y = 45 – 10 = 35. Aha! We're done.

ANSWER: b

5. As always, we start by making up numbers for the variables:
Each triangle's angles have to add up to 180°, so let's pick a=70, b= 70, c = 100, d=70 and e=70.
You might complain that we have assumed that the two upper triangles are isosceles. They don't have to be. If you like different angles, go ahead and pick them. Just make sure that each of your triangles have angles adding up to 180o. When you do, if you average your 5 angles, you will get the same thing I get: (70+70+70+70+100)/5=76.
ANSWER: 76

6. Start by making up the angles for a and c, but they have to add up to 200, so let's say a = 120 and c = 80. Then we can find the angles adjacent to a and c, inside the quadrilateral – each pair forms a line so each pair adds up to 180. That makes the two angles 60 and 100. Now we have a total of 160 and we need a total of 360, so the other two angles inside the quadrilateral could be 100 and 100 (or anything you like, but make them add up to 200). Finally, b and d each make a straight line with their inside neighbors, so that makes them 80 each. Then add them.
ANSWER: 160

Four Useful (though kind of dull) Facts about Triangles

OK, these may not be the most interesting SAT concepts that you will learn in this book. However, all of these have shown up on recent SATs, and they are quick to review.

1. In a single triangle, the longer side is opposite the bigger angle.

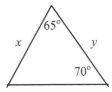

So if you look at the diagram, you can see that the side labeled x is across from the $70°$ angle. Since that is the biggest angle in this triangle, x must be the length of the longest side. So it's bigger than y.

2. The sum of the lengths of the two smaller sides of a triangle must be greater than the length of third side.

I always think of this as "The Drawbridge Rule". If the two short legs don't add up to more than the long one, the drawbridge won't close:

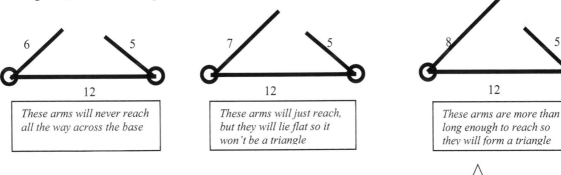

So, for example:

If m is a prime number, then the largest possible value for m is:

a) 5   b) 7   c) 9   d) 10   e) 11

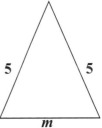

Figure not to scale

Well, to begin with, 9 is not prime ($9 = 3 \cdot 3$) and neither is 10 ($10 = 2 \cdot 5$).
And 11 is to big because of the drawbridge rule: $5 + 5 = 10$, so the third side must be less than 10. Both 5 and 7 are possible. And 7 is the larger of the two. So the answer is 'b'.

This idea appears in map problems where the sides of the triangles are distances between cities.

3. The longer side of a triangle has a shorter altitude.

In fact, they are inversely proportional. This means that if you multiply the length of any side by the length of its altitude, you get the same answer—you get twice the area of the triangle! That's why it's true: the area of the triangle is the same no matter which side you call the base -- as long as you use the height that goes with that base. So when you multiply them (and divide by 2) you get the same number. That means if one of them is bigger, the other must be smaller.

This is easier to understand if you look at this right triangle:

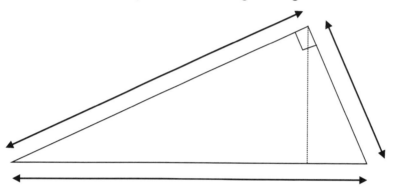

Now here's a trick question that's hard to get wrong: which side is the base?

One right answer: *The horizontal side or hypotenuse*

That is correct – but if you use that side as the base, you MUST use the dashed line inside the triangle as your height. The base and the height must be perpendicular.

Another right answer: *Either leg*

This is also correct and it is a better choice – you already have two sides that are perpendicular, so you might as well use one as the base and the other as the height.

So what's the point? Just this: suppose you use the hypotenuse as your base and I use the short leg as my base. Your hypotenuse is bigger than mine. But my height is bigger than yours. That's all I'm saying.

Does it always have to be that way? Why can't I have the bigger base AND the taller height?

Because we are still both talking about the same triangle. And when we calculate the area, we must get the same answer.

4. Similar Triangles – Use Ratios!

I have never seen the phrase "Similar triangles" on the SAT. They use the concept, but not the words. And you never have to prove that the two triangles are similar. So even if you had trouble with this in geometry class, you can still solve the SAT problems. Just make sure you can do the following two things.

i. *RECOGNIZE SIMILAR TRIANGLES WHEN YOU SEE THEM*

This is not too hard because the SAT uses the same two diagrams over and over:

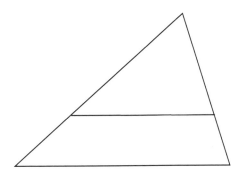

This is a triangle with a line drawn parallel to one of the sides. As a result, there are now TWO triangles. And the little one is similar to the big one.

And this is a "bow-tie". As long as the outside edges of the bow-tie are parallel, the two triangles will be similar.

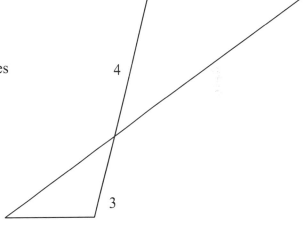

ii. *SOLVE BY USING RATIOS.*

"Similar" is a technical term. It means that the lengths of the sides of the triangles are proportional. That means you can set up ratios and solve for the unknowns as we did in the Ratio and Proportion section. I always do "little triangle is to big triangle as little triangle is to big".

So this time: $\dfrac{3}{4} = \dfrac{4}{x}$ which gives us $3x = 16$ and then $x = 16/3$ or 5.33.

Another example:

In the figure shown, segment PQ is parallel to segment AB. What is the value of x?

a) 5   b) 7   c) 8   d) 9   e) 10

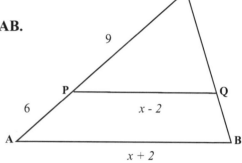

To solve this problem, you need to know that the little triangle is similar the big one. And you need to set up a proportion. But you do NOT need to do algebra. We can use trial and error with the answer choices (as you learned in Lesson #2).

Is x = 5?
Then the little triangle has sides 9 and 5 –2 = 3,
while the big triangle's sides are 9 + 6= 15 and 5 + 2 = 7.
But when you set up the ratios…

$\dfrac{9}{3} \neq \dfrac{15}{7}$ it doesn't work.

Is x = 7? Try it yourself…it doesn't work.

Is x = 8?
Then the little triangle has sides 9 and 8-2=6.
The big triangle has sides 15 and 8+2=10.
When you set up the ratios…

$\dfrac{9}{6} = \dfrac{15}{10}$ it works!

For those of you who <u>prefer</u> algebra…

You set up the equation:

$$\frac{9}{(x-2)} = \frac{15}{(x+2)}$$

and then cross-multiply, distribute, regroup and then solve.

That's all for this collection – except, of course, practice problems for you.

Practice Set #10: Four Useful Triangle Facts

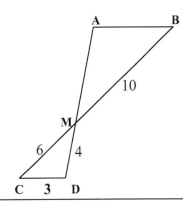

1. In the figure shown, AB is parallel to CD.
   What is the ratio of AM to MD?

a) 2:1   b) 3:2   c) 5:2   d) 5:3   e) 4:3

---

2. In the triangle shown, AC > BC. If AY = 7,
which of the following could be the length of BX?

a) 6.5   b) 7   c) 7.5   d) 8   e) 49

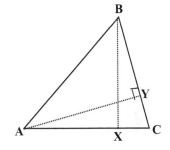

Questions 3 and 4 refer to the following:

You are given a collection of 5 sticks of the following lengths: 3 inches, 16 inches 20 inches, 34 inches and 50 inches.
Your goal is to take three of them and join them at their ends to make triangles.

3. Which of the sticks MUST be included among the three that you use?

a) the 3 inch   b) the 16 inch   c) the 20 inch and 34 inch   d) the 34 inch and 50 inch   e) the 50
inch

4. Which one of the sticks CANNOT be included among the three that you use?

a) the 3 inch   b) the 16 inch   c) the 20 inch   d) the 34 inch   e) the 50 inch

---

5. (A grid-in) If it is 10 miles between Smallville and Bedrock and 8 miles between Bedrock and Springfield, and
the three towns are NOT "co-linear" (they don't lie along a line on a map), what is one possible distance between
Smallville and Springfield?

---

6. Let x and y be the lengths of two sides of a triangle where $y = 2.5x$. Which of the following could NOT be the
length of the third side?

a) $2x$ b) y c) $(x + y)/2$ d) $2x + y$ e) $y - x$

Set #10: Answer Key

1. This is a typical similar-triangle-ratio problem. And the ratio is: $\dfrac{AM}{MD} = \dfrac{10}{6}$ which reduces to d) 5:3.

ANSWER: d

2. Since AC is GREATER than BC, it must have an altitude that is less than BC's altitude. BC's altitude is AY and the length of AY is given: it's 7. So BX must be less than 7, and there is only one answer choice that fits: a) 6.5 must be it!
NOTE: if you actually wanted to calculate BX with the information you've been given, it isn't possible. So once again, the student who knows to look at the answer choices and play around has a distinct advantage.
ANSWER: a

3. The two shorter sides you use must add up to longer than the third one. So here are the possible combinations:
    16, 20, 34   20, 34, 50
And, as you can see, the 20 inch stick is always used.
ANSWER: c

4. As you can also see from the explanation above, the 3 inch stick is never used.
ANSWER: a

5. Since these towns make are not on the same line, they form a triangle with sides 8 and 10. For your third side, you could pick any number MORE than 2 and less than 18.
ANSWER: 2 < answer < 18

6. Make up some numbers for x and y. I'll go with x = 10, y = 25. Now let's use the answers to get the possible third side and then check to see that the two smaller sides add to more than the big side:

a) x = 20 -- if the third side is 20, since 20 + 10 > 25, we are OK
b) y = 25 -- if the third side is 25, since 10 + 25 > 25, we are OK
c) (x+y)/2 = (10 + 25)/2 = 17.5 --if the third side is 17.5, since 10 + 17.5 > 25, we are OK
d) 2x + y = 20 + 25 = 45 but 10 + 25 is not greater than 45. SO THIS ONE CAN'T BE!
ANSWER: d

The Pythagorean Theorem (and Special Right Triangles)

I am sure that you learned this one in geometry class. It may very well be the single most famous math theorem ever:

$c^2 = a^2 + b^2$, where a and b are the legs and c is the hypotenuse of a right triangle.

And what if you have forgotten this theorem? Not to worry – it's printed on the front of every math section along with a bunch of other useful formulas. So how can this possibly be hard? Oh, they have their ways...

PYTHAGOREAN TRAP #1: The "missing" side is NOT always the hypotenuse.

Quick! What's the third side of this triangle:

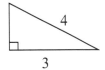

Most common wrong answer: 5

You can get the wrong answer two ways. If you set up the equation $c^2 = a^2 + b^2$, and then plugged in $c^2 = 3^2 + 4^2$, you get $c^2 = 25$, c= 5.

Or, you can just look at the numbers and remember that 3,4,5 is a Pythagorean triple. And you are right, it IS, but it does not apply to THIS triangle. The hypotenuse must be the longest side and in this triangle, the longest side's length is 4.

The right way is to start with the equation $c^2 = a^2 + b^2$ and then substitute $4^2 = 3^2 + b^2$, where one of the legs is the unknown. You get $16 = 9 + b^2$, so $b^2 = 7$ and then b = 2.65 (approximately).

You'll notice that I gave you the answer as a decimal approximation and not as $\sqrt{7}$. This leads us to the next trap.

PYTHAGOREAN TRAP #2: Simplifying Radicals – Don't do it!

In almost every right triangle problem, you have to take the square root of a number. So whoever taught you the Pythagorean theorem also had the unhappy task of teaching you how to simplify radicals and rationalize denominators. ***But there is no reason to do this on the SAT.*** You should use your calculator and get a decimal answer. Then, you'll notice that the SAT includes the decimal approximations in the answer choices, unless the choices are algebraic expressions. But you know what to do about that now. There's a back door.

For example...

If AB=BC=CD=DE, then AB=

a) x
b) $2x$
c) $\sqrt{2}x$
d) $2\sqrt{2}x$
e) $1.5x$

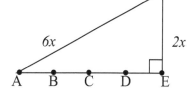

OK, the first thing we do here is get rid of the algebra. It's another back door problem. So we pick a number for x. I'll say x = 5. (You should try a different number, just to see it work.)

Now we have an easier problem. We just have to find the third side of a right triangle and then divide it by 4. (That's an extra twist. SAT problems are never exactly like school problems. There's always a twist...)

If we use x = 5, then the triangle is:

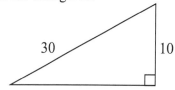

so we substitute into: $c^2 = a^2 + b^2$

and we get: $30^2 = 10^2 + b^2$,
$900 = 100 + b^2$

which we can solve for b: $800 = b^2$
$b = 28.28$

and then divide by 4 to get: AB= 7.07 This is <u>OUR</u> answer!

Of course, this does not look like any of <u>their</u> answers. But when you substitute OUR number (x=5) into each of the answer choices, you get:

a) 5
b) 10
c) 7.07 (a winner!)
d) 14.14
e) 7.5

Score another victory for the back door trick!

PYTHAGOREAN TRAP #3: Once is not enough!

If there are no other twists in the problem, the SAT will at least make you use the Pythagorean Theorem twice in the same problem. Try these two. I'll give you hints here and the answers are on the bottom of the next page.

Determine the length of segment AB.

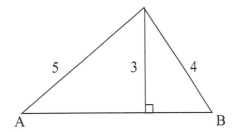

Hints: You cannot just use the Pythagorean Theorem on the outside triangle because it isn't a right triangle. But you can work on the left-side triangle and then the right-side triangle, find the missing leg for each of them, and then add them together. By the way, the one on the left IS a 3,4,5 right triangle. The one on the right is NOT. If you don't know why, re-read Trap #1.

Determine the length, _x_.

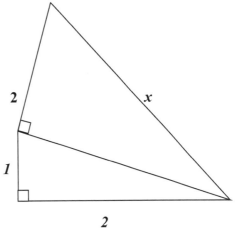

Hint: Use the Pythagorean Theorem on the lower triangle to find its hypotenuse. Then, the hypotenuse of that triangle is a leg of the triangle above it. So now you can use the Pythagorean Theorem again…

One more note…

The Pythagorean Theorem is often one step in a bigger problem about area and shaded regions, which we'll get to soon. But first, there's one more Pythagorean trap…

Pythagorean Trap #4: Special Right Triangles

What are they? What's so special about them? Let's take a look:

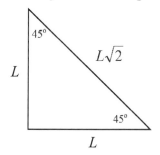
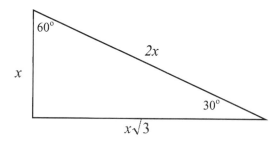

Here we have a 45-45-90 triangle and a 30-60-90 triangle, each named after its angles.

What's special is that if you know the length of any one side, you can find the lengths of the other two sides, just by memorizing a bunch of rules. And oh, how we hate these! 45-45-90 and 30-60-90 triangles are as much fun to learn about as they are to teach. Which is to say, not very much fun at all. Please, oh please, can't we find a way to deal with these? Hmm…I can help you here, by giving you some options. It's up to you to choose which option works best for you.

Option #1: Don't bother!

If you really can't stand these, you can skip them. They don't show up on every SAT, and when they do, it's usually later in the section, which may even be outside of your zone. Also, sometimes you can just work things out by using the Pythagorean theorem. So if this topic was your particular nightmare in geometry, feel free to let it go.

Option #2: Use the information in the front of the section to help memorize some rules.

The diagrams above are included in the front of each math section. They can be used to remind you of the following rules:

45-45-90

$$hypotenuse = leg \cdot \sqrt{2}$$

30-60-90

$$shortest = hypotenuse / 2$$

$$medium = shortest \cdot \sqrt{3}$$

This is probably the option your math teacher would choose. But if you are not already comfortable with these rules, they are really not worth memorizing now. The return on your investment is not great enough to make it worth your time. However, there is a chance that you already know another way to do this, if you have already learned a little bit of trigonometry.

ANSWERS TO PROBLEMS FROM PREVIOUS PAGE:

1. The missing leg for the triangle on the left has length 4 The missing leg for the triangle on the right has length $\sqrt{7}$. Then, you just have to add. **ANSWER:** $4 + \sqrt{7}$

2. The hypotenuse of the lower triangle is $\sqrt{5}$. Then, use that to find the hypotenuse of the upper triangle. **ANSWER: 3**

Option #3: Use Right-Triangle-Trigonometry (SOHCAHTOA)

Officially, there is no trigonometry on the SAT. That means that there is no problem that <u>requires</u> the use of trigonometry. But that doesn't mean it isn't allowed. And in the case of special right triangles, trigonometry makes things easier.

HOWEVER, if you have never learned the basic trigonometric ratios (SOHCAHTOA), you'd be better off sticking with option #1 (skip it) or option #2 (the school way).

The easiest way for me to explain is with an example:

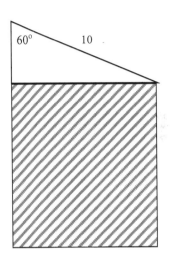

Find the area of the shaded square.

Well a square's area is easy when you know the length of a side. But we don't know a side just yet. We do know one side of a special triangle, though. And your math teachers would say something like:

"Thus, the shorter side is half the hypotenuse, which is 5, and then the middle length side, which is opposite the 60° angle, is $5\sqrt{3}$, which we then square to find the area of the shade region."

And, of course, this is all entirely correct. I just don't think it's the method most students are comfortable with. If you know the trig, here's what I think is easier:

The length we need is **o**pposite 60°, and the length we know is the **h**ypotenuse. So the trig ratio we use is the sine. (Sine=opposite/hypotenuse is the SOH in SOHCAHTOA).

We get: $\dfrac{opposite}{10} = \sin 60°$ or $\dfrac{x}{10} = .866$ so $x = 8.66$, which is the length of the side.

Then, we square it to get the area: $8.66^2 = 75$ and we are done.

Option #4: Use the law of sines.

But if you have not already learned this, I don't recommend it (and I'm not explaining it here). But for those of you who DO know it, you may not have realized that it works in this setting. It does.

I would not be surprised if after all this, you go back to Option #1 (skip it). Oh, well. I admit that I have trouble finding a way to make this particular topic easy or fun. You can't win 'em all. But you can win a lot of them. So try the practice problems and see if you win a few.

Practice Set # 11: Pythagorean Theorem Problems

1. A right triangle has one vertex at the origin, a second vertex at (24,0) and the third vertex at (24,k) where $k > 0$. If the length of the hypotenuse is 25, what is the value of k?

   a) 1   b) 7   c) 12   d) 24   e) 25

2. On his walk to school, Sam goes around the outside edges of a rectangular field that is 100 feet long and 50 feet wide, walking along one long side and one short side. On some days, he cuts across the field diagonally. Approximately how much shorter is his trip to school when he uses that shortcut?

   a) No shorter at all   b) 12 feet   c) 38 feet   d) 75 feet   e) 112 feet

3. Let $a \, \mathcal{H} \, b$ be defined, for all a and b greater than zero, as the length of the hypotenuse of the right triangle which has a and b as the lengths of its two legs. Which of the following is equal to $24 \, \mathcal{H} \, 7$?

a) $7 \, \mathcal{H} \, 11$ b) $12.5 \, \mathcal{H} \, 12.5$ c) $10 \, \mathcal{H} \, 15$ d) $1 \, \mathcal{H} \, 25$ e) $15 \, \mathcal{H} \, 20$

4. (A grid-in) The figure below shows two right triangles. Find the length, x:

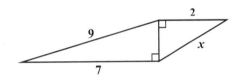

5. (A grid-in) The right triangle shown below has an area equal to $18\sqrt{3}$. Determine the length of its hypotenuse.

6. (A grid-in)   Find the area of the shaded square.

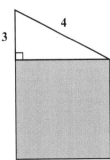

117

Set #11: Answer Key

NOTE FOR PROBLEMS 1 – 3:

Each of these takes a straightforward right triangle problem and puts a little twist on it. That's how the SAT does it too.

1. After you draw a neat diagram, you can see that this is just a Pythagorean Theorem problem. You know that the length of the hypotenuse is 25 and one leg is 24. So $a^2 + 24^2 = 25^2$ and when you solve, you get a=7. But in this case, a represents the y-coordinate of the third vertex, (24,k). That means k=7.
ANSWER: b

2. If you walk around the outside, you have to walk 100 feet and then 50 feet for a total of 150 feet. The diagonal is the length of the hypotenuse, found by using: $100^2 + 50^2 = c^2$. You get c = 111.8 – but then you have to subtract that from 150 to find how much shorter the shortcut is: 150 – 111.8 = 38.2, or approximately 38.
ANSWER: c

3. First, find the hypotenuse when the legs are 24 and 7: $24^2 + 7^2 = c^2$, and you should get c=25. Now, check each answer choice one at a time, looking for another pair that also has a hypotenuse of 25. When you finally try choice 'e', you get: $15^2 + 20^2 = c^2$ and c = 25. [More on these "funny symbol" problems later]
ANSWER: e

4. Now, we are going to make you use the Pythagorean Theorem twice.
First: $7^2 + b^2 = 9^2$, from which you can solve that b = 5.6568…
Then, $b^2 + 2^2 = x^2$, which gives you 32 +4 = x^2, and you can solve that x = 6.
ANSWER: 6

5. First of all, if you hate this kind of question, remember that one good strategy is to just skip it. It's HARD. For those of you who are brave, or stubborn, here goes:
It would seem that they have not given us enough information. We know the area, and if they would tell us the base, we could get the height, or if they told us the height, we could get the base. But it seems that all we are given is the area. But wait…they also give us the angles. This is a 30-60-90 triangle. The height is half the hypotenuse and the base is the height x $\sqrt{3}$. And if you multiply those, and divide your answer in half, you get $18\sqrt{3}$. So before you divide in half, it was $36\sqrt{3}$. That means the height was 6 and the base was $6\sqrt{3}$. Then, with the base and height, you can use the Pythagorean theorem to get the hypotenuse. Of course, you don't have to do that—the height is half the hypotenuse, so the hypotenuse is 12. Lovely.
ANSWER: 12

6. Boy, compared to the last one, this is a walk in the park. Use $3^2 + x^2 = 4^2$, solve for x, and you get x = 2.65, so clearly, the area is x^2 which is…
ANSWER: 7

Areas, including Shaded-Region problems

Here's the plan: you learn how to find the areas of FOUR basic shapes. Three of the four are listed in the front of each math section, but you are going to memorize them anyway. Then, once you know the basic shapes, you have to practice putting them together. Finally, you have to learn how to see shaded areas as one region taken away from another. There are only a handful of variations on this central theme so a little bit of practice goes a long way.

The Basic Shapes:

1. Rectangle: Area = length x width

   (and if it happens to be a square, then of course, the length and width are the same.)

2. Triangle: Area = ½ base x height

   (where the height is the perpendicular distance from a given base to the opposite vertex)

   Caution: DO NOT FORGET TO DIVIDE BY 2 AFTER YOU MULTIPLY!
   I know this is a common error because usually one of the answer choices is what you get if you don't divide. If you are willing to make this mistake, they are willing to trap you.

   Sneaky trick: If two triangles have the same base and same height, then they have the same area, even if they look different, like the two in this diagram:

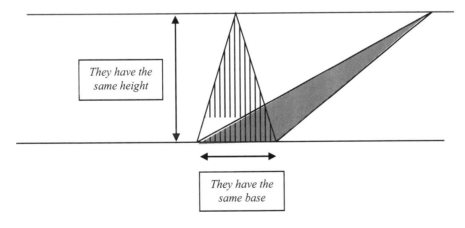

On the other hand…
   If the bases are the same, then the taller triangle has the bigger area.
   If the heights are the same, then the wider triangle has the bigger area.

119

3.   Circle: Area = πr^2

(NOT $2\pi r$...that's the circumference. But if you forget, you can look it up in the front.)

4.   Partial Circle: The area of the partial circle is the same fraction of the whole circle that the central angle is out of 360°.

You can write this as an equation:

Area of sector = $\pi r^2 \cdot \dfrac{n}{360}$, where n is the measure of the central angle.

Or you might find it easier to think of sectors this way:

Start with πr^2. That's the area of the entire circle.
Now take 360 and divide it by whatever the central angle is. So say the angle is 20°.
You'll divide 360 by 20 and get 18. So if you divide the area of the whole circle by 18, you get the area of the sector.

It is also worth it to just know a few commonly encountered partial circles by heart:

Semi-circle (n=180°)   Quarter Circle (n=90°)   Sixth of a circle (n=60°)

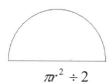

$\pi r^2 \div 2$ $\pi r^2 \div 4$ $\pi r^2 \div 6$

And that's the whole collection. All of the area problems on the SAT are built on these shapes, so if you know these formulas, you are well on your way. However, and by now you are probably expecting this, the SAT has its own unique way of twisting these problems. By far, the most common way is by asking you to find "the shaded region". So let's take a look at a handful of them.

The Shaded Region

When you need to find the area of some region, stay calm and remember that the region is always built from the four basic shapes. Either the shapes have been joined together...

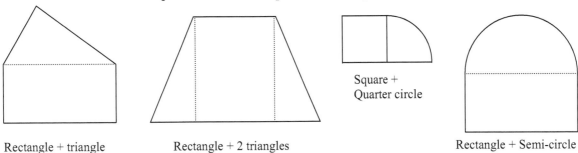

Rectangle + triangle   Rectangle + 2 triangles   Square +
Quarter circle

Rectangle + Semi-circle

...or there is a shaded region that you find by <u>subtracting</u> one area from another.

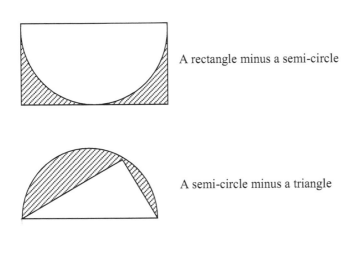

A rectangle minus a semi-circle

A semi-circle minus a triangle

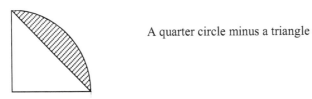

A quarter circle minus a triangle

Of course, these are not the only possible combinations. But they give you the idea. They are complicated shapes, until you see that they are just the basic shapes, put together or taken apart. But once you see that, now what do you do? You write down the formulas for the basic shapes, fill in the given information, and calculate your answer in decimal form. Then, pick the answer that matches.

"OK, suppose I memorize my basic shapes and the formulas that go with them. Will I always be given enough information to find the areas I need?"

Yes. But you may have to work past one of the following obstacles:

1. The dimensions you need may be given as algebraic variables. And then the answer choices will have variables as well. Hmmm. Variables in the question, variables in the answers. Back Door!

2. You may think you are missing one key piece of information. But it turns out that this problem also involves a right triangle, and the Pythagorean Theorem will give you that missing piece.

3. You may think you are missing one key piece of information. But it turns out that this problem also involves a circle whose radius you know – and the side you are missing is another radius of the same circle. The SAT loves this trick. I call it the "every-radius" trick and I have included it in some of the examples that follow.

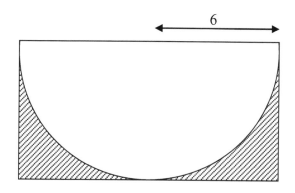

A semi-circle of radius 6 is inscribed in a rectangle, as shown. Determine the area of the shaded region.

As we have seen, this shaded region is a rectangle minus a semi-circle. So to find its area, we will be calculating:

Length x width $- \pi r^2/2$,

as soon as we figure out the length, width and radius. Now they radius is easy: it's 6. (They told us in the text of the problem and on the diagram.) But it seems as if they forgot to tell us the length and width of the rectangle. Of course, they didn't really forget. The circle has radius of 6, so every radius is 6. From that fact, we can quickly deduce that the length is 12 and the width is 6. So the area we are looking for is:

$12 \text{x} 6 - \pi 6^2/2 = 15.45$

Let's try another. This time, I will walk you through it:

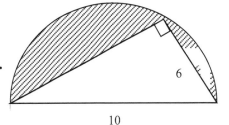

A right triangle is inscribed in a semicircle, as shown. The area of the shaded region is:

a) $50\pi - 30$
b) $25\pi - 30$
c) $12.5\pi - 48$
d) $12.5\pi - 24$
e) $50\pi - 24$

If you have trouble with any step, the answers are on the bottom of the next page.

Step 1: What shapes do you have to add or subtract?

Step 2: What are the formulas for those shapes?

Step 3: Do you have the dimensions you need?
　　　　Hints: The radius is <u>half</u> the diameter.
　　　　　　　And you will need the Pythagorean theorem…

Step 4: Calculate the areas of the two shapes, and then subtract.

One additional note about this problem:

If you are a very sharp math student, you may have noticed that they didn't have to tell us that this is a right triangle. Every triangle inscribed in a semi-circle is a right triangle. (The measure of an inscribed angle is half of the measure of the intercepted arc.) But the SAT does not require you to know that fact. They give you the right angle. But congratulations to you anyway if you noticed this. (And no big deal if you did not.)

123

And here is one more example of the "every-radius" trick. It's an old geometry teacher's puzzle, but it still shows up on the SAT now and then. You do not need a calculator:

Point C is the center of a circle.
ABCD is a rectangle.
AD=5 and AC=3.
Find length CE.

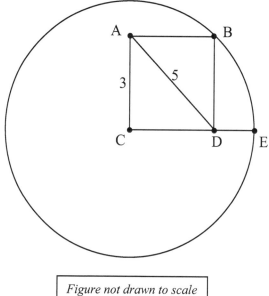

Figure not drawn to scale

Give yourself a little while to figure this one out before you read the hints…

Hints: Are you sure you want a hint already? Do you want to try a little longer on your own? No? Are you sure? OK. Here come the hints…

1. That the length AC = 3 is irrelevant. If you used it to solve for CD = 4, it then makes you focus your attention on finding DE so that you can add it to CD to get your answer. But that is NOT how to solve this one, even though it is a reasonable start. I told you this one was tricky!

2. The length you need, CE, is actually a <u>radius</u> of this circle. Maybe we can find that radius by finding some OTHER radius since, after all, EVERY RADIUS is the same.

3. Hmm. What would be a good radius to try to find? How about CB?

OK, that's all the hints you get!

(And yes, I know that this problem goes beyond tricky into the realm of the obnoxious. You are not a better student or college candidate because you know the trick. But you ARE a better math SAT taker. Isn't that why you are still reading?)

Step 1: The shaded region is a semi-circle minus a triangle.
Step 2: It's $\pi r^2/2 - \frac{1}{2}$ bh
Step 3: The radius is 5. Using the Pythagorean Theorem, we can find that the other side of the triangle is 8. So then we can use 8 as the base and 6 as the height.
Step 4: $25\pi/2 - \frac{1}{2} 6\cdot8 = 12.5\pi - 24$… 'd'

Practice Set # 12: Area and the Shaded Region

1. (A grid-in)

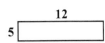

Find the ratio of the rectangle's area to that of the right triangle.

2. The diagram at right shows a figure whose boundaries are three semi-circles. The line segment AB has length 8. The area enclosed by the three semi-circles is:

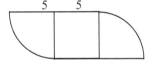

a) 12π b) 16π c) 32π d) 48π e) 64π

3. Both of the curves in the figure shown are arcs of circles. Which of the following is the best approximation for the area of the figure?

a) 44.6   b) 50.0   c) 64.3   d) 78.5   e) 196.3

4. In the figure shown, a right triangle is inscribed in a quarter circle. If the radius of the circle is r, then the area of the shaded region is:

a) $r^2\left(\frac{1}{2} - \frac{\pi}{4}\right)$

b) $r^2\left(\frac{1}{4} - \frac{\pi}{2}\right)$

c) $r^2\left(\frac{\pi}{2} - \frac{1}{2}\right)$

d) $r^2\left(\frac{\pi}{4} - \frac{1}{2}\right)$

e) $r^2\left(1 - \frac{\pi}{4}\right)$

5. (A grid-in) Determine the area of the figure shown at right.

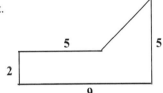

6. (A Grid-in) The sector of the circle shown has a radius of 6 and an area of 3π. What is the measure of angle ABO?

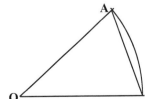

Set #12: Answer Key

1. OK, the rectangle area is easy: 5x12=60. But you have to apply the Pythagorean Theorem to find the missing side of the right triangle. When you do, you get $5^2 + x^2 = 13^2$ and that comes out to x = 12. So the are of the triangle is ½ 5 x 12 or 30. Then the ration is 60: 30 or…
ANSWER: 2

2. We need to add up the areas of the two little semicircles and the one big one. The radius of the big semicircle is 4 because the radius is half of the length AB. Then, the radii of the little circles are each half of 4, or 2. So the overall area is: $½ \pi 4^2 + ½ \pi 2^2 + ½ \pi 2^2 = 12\pi$
ANSWER: a

3. This time, we are adding up a square and 2 quarter circles, or one half circle. The area of the square is 5 x 5 = 25. The area of the half circle is $½ \pi 5^2 = 12.5\pi$. Add it up and you get 25 + 12.5π. = 64.3
ANSWER: c

4. First, pick a value for r. I used r = 10. Then, we have a quarter circle minus a triangle. The area of the quarter circle is: $¼ \pi 10^2 = 25\pi$. The area of the triangle = ½ x 10 x 10 = 50. Subtract and you get the shaded region: $25\pi - 50 = 28.5$.

Then, substitute r = 10 into each answer choice. The only match is d) $r^2(\frac{\pi}{4} - \frac{1}{2})$.

ANSWER: d

5. This is easy when you break it down. The dashed line shows you how: (And the length of the dashed segment = 4.)
Then, it's just a rectangle: A = 9 x 2 = 18
And a triangle: A = ½ 4 x 3 = 6.
So the total area = 24.
ANSWER: 24

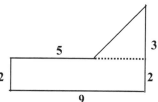

6. This one is tricky. First you have to find the central angle AOB. The circle of radius 6 would have an area of $\pi 6^2$ which is 36π. The sector has an area of only 3π. So the central angle must be 3/36ths (or 1/12th) of a circle, which is 1/12th of 360°, or 30°. But wait. We're still not done. We have not found the angle that they asked for, and it doesn't look like we have enough information. But we do—it's the "every-radius" trick…that triangle must be isosceles! So the two missing angles are the same, and together with the 30° angle, they add up to 180°. So they must be 75° each. I told you it was tricky.
ANSWER: 75

Round 3 – Algebra II

These are the big, scary advanced topics that the SAT added a few years ago. I am presenting them in the order that makes sense to me, but that is not the same as the order of importance in terms of how often this stuff appears on the SAT. In that department, FUNCTIONS would definitely be the most important, so go especially slow when you hit that section.

The topics are:

> Exponents
> Functions
> Coordinate Geometry and Slope
> More on Graphs: Lines and Parabolas

Exponents

First of all, make sure you know how to enter exponents on your calculator. On most calculators, the exponent symbol is ^ but on some, it is a little button that says y^x – either way, check that you know what to do.

Then, here are the basic rules you must know:

1. To multiply exponents with a common base, add the exponents. For example:

$$5^2 \times 5^3 = 5^5$$

But why? Well, reason #1 is that if you try it on your calculator, you'll see that it's true. But if you want a better reason:

$$5^2 = 5 \times 5 \text{ and } 5^3 = 5 \times 5 \times 5 \text{ so } 5^2 \times 5^3 = (5 \times 5) \times (5 \times 5 \times 5) = 5^5$$

(To divide exponents with a common base, you subtract the exponents – but I have not seen this on the SAT yet.)

2. To raise an exponent to a higher exponent, you multiply the exponents. For example:

$$(5^2)^3 = 5^6$$

And the reason this time is: $(5^2)^3 = (5 \times 5)^3 = (5 \times 5)(5 \times 5)(5 \times 5) = 5^6$

3. Negative exponents are inverses. This one takes too long to explain. But your calculator will tell you that it's true. Use your calculator to check that these are right:

$$5^{-1} = \frac{1}{5} = .2 \qquad \text{and} \qquad 2^{-3} = \frac{1}{2^3} = \frac{1}{8} = .125$$

4. Fractional exponents are roots. But so far on the SAT, I've only seen the fraction ½ used as an exponent. And it means "positive square root". So for example:

$$81^{\frac{1}{2}} = 9 \text{ ...and if we want to try a tricky one: } 81^{-\frac{1}{2}} = \frac{1}{81^{\frac{1}{2}}} = \frac{1}{9}$$

Practice Set #13: Exponents

1. If $a^{2b} = a^{b+1}$ and $a > 1$, which of the following MUST be true?

a) $b = 0$ b) $b = \frac{1}{2}$ c) $b = 1$ d) $a = b$ e) $b = 2a$

2. If $(7^x)(7^y)(7^z) = 7^{12}$, what is the average of x, y and z?

a) 3   b) 4   c) 6   d) 12   e) 36

3. Which of the following must be the length of one side of a square that has an area of w?

       I. $w/4$ II. $\sqrt{w}$ III. $w^{\frac{1}{2}}$

a) I only   b) II only   c) II and III   d) I and III   e) I, II and III

4. Given that $k^{-1} = .2$ and $m^{1/2} = k$, find the value of m.

a) -.4   b) -.8   c) 2.5   d) 10   e) 25

5. (A Grid-in) If $6^x \div 6^y = 36$ then what is the value of $2x - 2y$?

6. (A Grid-in) $\dfrac{1}{4^{-1}} - (3^2)^{\frac{1}{2}} = ?$

Set# 13: Answer Key

1. You could do this one by recognizing that since the bases are the same, the powers have to be the same as well. This means that $2b = b + 1$ which algebra or trial and error then reveals to be true when $b = 1$.
Answer: c

2. Since we are multiplying and the bases are all the same, we can add the exponents. This tells us that $x + y + z = 12$. So at this point, why not make up numbers that add up to 12? Being extremely lazy, I'll go with 4, 4 and 4. (12, 0 and 0 would also be admirably lazy). Then, I take the average of my numbers. $(4 + 4 + 4)/3 = 4$.
Answer: b

3. There are two things you need to know to get this right:
1. The side is the square root of the area
2. An exponent of ½ is the same as a square root.
Answer: c

4. If $1/k = .2$, then $k = 5$ (trial and error, algebra or TI89). So now we are looking for m, and we know that its square root is 5. Aha, m=25.
Answer: e

5. You could just play around with different numbers on your calculator until you find an x and a y that make it work. For example, x=3 and y=1. Or x=4 and y=2. Most kids who get this right are going to do it that way. OR, you could notice that $36=6^2$, and that when you divide, you subtract exponents, so $x - y = 2$. That makes it easier to find pairs of numbers that fit. I'll go with x=3, y=1. Then, $2x - 2y = 6 - 2 = 4$.
Answer: 4

6. OK, if you are careful here, you can just enter the expression into your calculator. Your calculator knows how to do exponents and it knows its order of operations. But if you prefer, you can also do this by hand: 4^{-1} is ¼ and $1/(¼) = 4$. $3^2=9$ and the square root of 9 = 3. $4 - 3 = 1$.
Answer: 1

What is the SAT's FUNCTION?

Warning: This is a BIG DEAL on the SAT. And of all the topics in this book, this is the one that scares kids most. But you CANNOT afford to skip the function problems – some SATs have four or five of them! So read this section CAREFULLY and work your way slowly through the exercises until you get this figured out.

A function is a way of assigning one number to another. In school, they call it a "mapping". Another good way to think of a function is as a machine – a machine that matches one number with another.

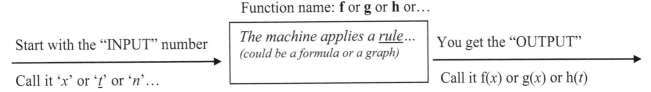

When you read an SAT problem about functions, it is important to be able to recognize what information you are being given. So I'm going to give you a typical function problem and we are going to break it down (like diagramming a sentence in English class).

Let the function f be defined by... *(here comes the rule)...*

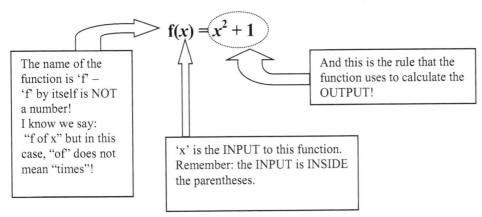

Now there are two different ways that this problem could go...we'll start with the easier way...

Find: f(9) = ?   The input is 9. So we put 9 into the rule. $9^2 + 1 = 82$

Find: $\dfrac{1}{f(\frac{1}{2}) - 1} = ?$ The input is $\dfrac{1}{2}$. So we find $\left(\dfrac{1}{2}\right)^2 + 1 = 1.25$ and then $\dfrac{1}{1.25 - 1} = \dfrac{1}{.25} = 4$

Though the second problem is a little harder than the first, they still both come down to the same idea: here is a function, we give you the INPUT and you have to find the OUTPUT. You do this by applying the rule, using the INPUT in place of the 'x' (or the 't' or whatever letter they used).

131

And here's the OTHER way they could have gone with this problem:

Let the function *f* be defined by *f(x)* = x^2 + 1.

If *f(a)* = 10 and *a* < 0, then *a* = ???

The important thing here is to understand what NOT to do. The answer is NOT:

$a = 10^2 + 1 = 101$

This can't be right…101 is not less than 0. That tells us we did something wrong. Look again:

If f(a) = 10… WHICH ONE IS THE INPUT?!? It's not 10. It's 'a'! Some unknown value called 'a' is the input and 10 is the output. So we have to apply the rule to that unknown input. When we do, we get:

$a^2 + 1 = 10$ which you have to solve by…ALGEBRA or TRIAL & ERROR or TI-89
but remember, we are looking for a negative answer (because a<0).

(Answer is below.)[*]

So be on the alert:

Did they give me the INPUT and ask for the OUTPUT or did they give me the OUTPUT and ask for the INPUT?

The INPUT is inside the parentheses.

Do they always give you one or the other? Yes, and sometimes they give you BOTH as you will see in the next example.

---

[*] It's *a* = -3

The Case of the Missing Constant

In some problems, when you are up to the point where they give you the output rule, you find that the formula has an unknown constant in it. For example:

Let the function g be defined by $g(t) = bt - t^2$. If $g(4) = 24$, find b.

OK, let's start by diagramming the sentence:

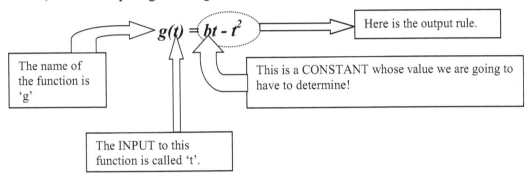

Whenever there is an unknown constant in the rule for the function's output, you can be sure of two things:

1. They are going to ask YOU to find the value of the constant.
2. They are going to give you the INPUT and the OUTPUT, both!

So, to continue the problem...

g(4) = 24   This means that when you use 4 as the INPUT you get 24 as the OUTPUT.

Applying the rule for the function, you get: $b \times 4 - 4^2 = 24$

And again, it's your choice: algebra, trial & error or TI-89.[*]

Now there's one more function trick you need to know: sometimes, you are not given a formula for the rule, and you are still expected to find the output from the input or the input from the output. But this time, all you are given is a graph of the function. And what you are going to discover is that it's easier when you have a graph, once you know what to do.

You should get $b=10$

133

FUNCTIONS AND GRAPHS

You already know how to graph points on the plane. For example, the diagram shows the point (5,2) and you can see that it is 5 "over" and 2 "up". That's why (a,b) is called and "ordered pair" – the order matters. And as for why the first value is the value along the x-axis and the second value is the y-axis value, well that could have been done either way, but what matters is that we all agree to do it the same way (which we do: x first, y second).

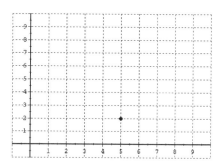

Well, a long time ago, a mathematician had a great idea: we can make ordered pairs out of the inputs and outputs of a function. Then we can graph them and it will give us a picture of what the function looks like. We just have to decide what order to use. But again, it's not up to us – the decision has already been made and it's: (Input, Output).

So from now on, for the purpose of function problems on the SAT...

1. The x-axis is called "The Input Axis"

2. The y-axis is called "The Output Axis".

Once you understand how this works, these problems will seem MUCH easier. You just have to count boxes.

Let *h(t)* be defined for -1 <t < 6.
The graph of h is shown at right.

Find *h*(2).

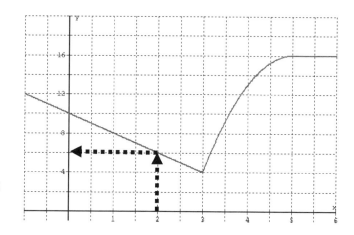

So what do we do here? Just follow along:

1. Start on the x-axis at x=2
2. Go up to the graph of the function.
3. Go over to the y-axis and read the value! It's 6. And that's the answer.

To help you see what I mean, I've drawn arrows on the graph. On the SAT, you'll have to do that yourself.

Now you try this one, still using the same graph. The answer is at the bottom of the next page.

Find *h*(4) – *h*(1).

134

But what if they give me the output?

Then you just do the same process, but in reverse, starting on the y-axis, going <u>over</u> to the graph of the function and then <u>down</u> to the x-axis. For example:

If *h(m)* = 4, then *m* = ?

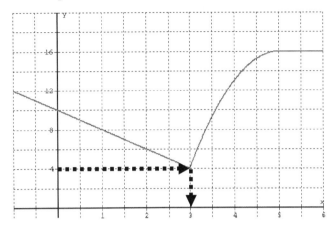

Again, follow the arrows…

1. Start on the y-axis at y=4
2. Go over to the graph
3. Go down to the x-axis and read the value. It's 3, and that's the answer.

And one last twist…

If *h(k)* = 8, find the sum of all possible values of *k*.

With this one, you start at the y-axis at y=8. But then, when you are heading over to the graph, there is more than one place where you can stop. That can happen with functions. This time, there are TWO inputs that give 8 as the output. They are x=1 and x=3.3 (approximately). How do you know which one to use? You READ THE QUESTION! It says to give the sum of all possible values, so you add them.

Now that you understand graphs of functions, let's take a look at some of the ways that the graphs can be changed. Because, as we all know…

It's h(4)=13 and h(1) = 8 and then 13 – 8 = 5

Shifts Happen. (Stretches and Flips also Happen.)

You need to know what would happen to the graph if we change the function in some minor way. But before we look at examples, I want to give you a general rule about the changes we make and the results they produce:

Changes OUTSIDE the parentheses affect the graph VERTICALLY.
Changes INSIDE the parentheses affect the graph HORIZONTALLY - - and act the opposite way.

In each pair of graphs below, the solid line is the original function, f(x) and the dashed line is the new function, after we made the change listed next to each graph.

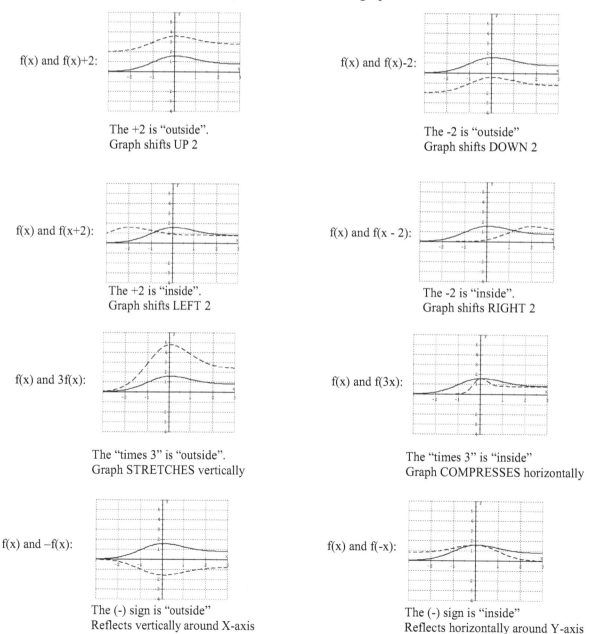

f(x) and f(x)+2:

The +2 is "outside".
Graph shifts UP 2

f(x) and f(x)-2:

The -2 is "outside"
Graph shifts DOWN 2

f(x) and f(x+2):

The +2 is "inside".
Graph shifts LEFT 2

f(x) and f(x - 2):

The -2 is "inside".
Graph shifts RIGHT 2

f(x) and 3f(x):

The "times 3" is "outside".
Graph STRETCHES vertically

f(x) and f(3x):

The "times 3" is "inside"
Graph COMPRESSES horizontally

f(x) and –f(x):

The (-) sign is "outside"
Reflects vertically around X-axis

f(x) and f(-x):

The (-) sign is "inside"
Reflects horizontally around Y-axis

Practice Set #14: Functions

Note: NONE of these are easy. Sorry.

1. Let the function f be defined by $f(x) = 3x + 1$. If $f(a)=10$, what is the value of $f(3a)$?

a) 3   b) 9   c) 10   d) 28   e) 30

2. (A Grid-in) A ball is launched upward from the ground at a speed of v feet per second. Its height as a function of time is given by the formula: $h(t) = v \cdot t - 16t^2$. If the height after 4 seconds is 24 feet, determine the value of the launch speed, v, in feet/second.

3. If $g(1) = -1$ and $g(-1) = 1$, which of the following could be the definition of the function g?

a) $g(t) = t - 2$ b) $g(t) = t + 2$ c) $g(t) = -t^2$ d) $g(t) = 1 - t$ e) $g(t) = -t$

The next three questions are all based on the following definitions:

Let f be defined by the equation $f(x) = 10 - 2x$ and let h be the function whose graph is shown.

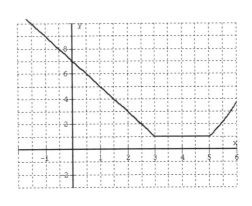

4. If $h(m)=5$ and $m > 0$, then m is most nearly…

a) 4   b) 5   c) 7   d) 9   e) undefined

5. Determine the value of $h(f(5))$.

a) 0   b) 2   c) 4   d) 5   e) 8

6. Which function has the graph shown at right:

a) $h(x - 2) - 1$
b) $h(x + 2) - 1$
c) $h(x - 2) + 1$
d) $h(x - 1) + 2$
e) $h(x - 1) + 2$

Set #14: Answer Key

1. We know the function: $f(x) = 3x + 1$. And we know the OUTPUT is 10. So by trial and error or by algebra, we figure out that the INPUT is 3 (because $3 \times 3 + 1 = 10$). So $a = 3$. Then, $3a = 9$. And then finally, $f(9) = 3 \times 9 + 1 = 28$

Answer: d

2. This looks like you need to know some physics, but you definitely do NOT. You just need to know how to solve the case of the missing constant. In the formula $h(t) = v \cdot t - 16t^2$, v is an unknown constant. So they are going to have to give you an INPUT and an OUTPUT. The input is 4 seconds and the output is 24 feet. That means:

$24 = v \cdot 4 - 16 \cdot 4^2$, and equation we can solve by trial and error, TI89 or algebra. By algebra, it's:
$24 = 4v - 256$
$280 = 4v$
$70 = v$

Answer: 70

3. The easiest way to solve this one is to use 1 as the input and rule out any answer choice that does not give -1 as the output. That narrows it down to a, c and e. Then use -1 as the input and see which of those three choices gives +1 as the output.

Answer: e

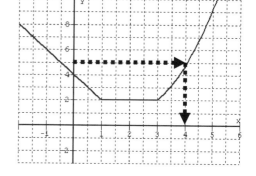

4. If $h(m)=5$ and $m > 0$, then m is most nearly...

Follow the arrows...
...from the output axis, to the graph, to the input axis.
Answer: a

5. Determine the value of $h(f(5))$:
This one is tricky. FIRST you have to find $f(5)$.
The rule is $f(x) = 10 - 2x$, so $f(5) = 10 - 2 \times 5 = 0$.

Then, for $h(0)$, you have to go to the graph, start at 0 on the x-axis and go up to the graph, where y=4.
Answer: c

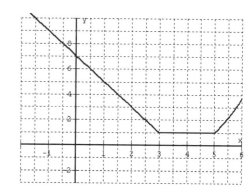

6. Compare the graph to the original graph.
You can see that it has been shifted DOWN 1.
And it has been shifted RIGHT 2. So it's -1 OUTSIDE and -2 INSIDE -- $h(x - 2) - 1$
Answer: a

Coordinate Geometry and Slope

Coordinate Geometry is just a fancy name for everything related to plotting points on the (x, y) plane. The SAT requires you to know a tiny bit about this. And there is an amazingly simple, common sense trick that makes all of these problems easier:

If the problem has <u>anything</u> to do with graphing points, take the time to draw your own graph paper. Be as neat as you can be. Then, find the distances you need by COUNTING THE BOXES!!!

Here is an example that I will do for you:

The diameter of a circle has its endpoints located at (-2, -1) and (8, -1). If (3, k) is also a point on the circle and k > 0, then k=…

a) 3   b) 4   c) 5   d) 6   e) 7

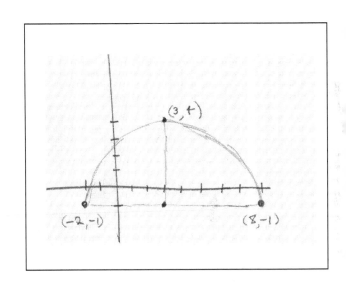

First I draw my own graph paper, and I neatly label the points. (You can see from my diagram that you don't have to be perfect – just neat.)

Then, I can count boxes and find the diameter is 10, so the radius is 5. Also, I can see that an x-value of 3 is midway between the endpoints.

And, since <u>every</u> radius must be 5, I count 5 units up and I land on a y-value of 4. (I counted up and not down because k>0.)

Now you try this next one. I'll make it a grid-in question.

If (c, 0) is a point on the segment with endpoints at A(0,2) and B(5,-2) find the largest integer that is less than c.

The solution is on the next page, but don't peek until you have made your own neat diagram. You'll see that this is easier than it looks.

OK, it said:

**(c, 0) is a point on the segment with
endpoints at A(0,2) and B(5,-2)**

So we draw:

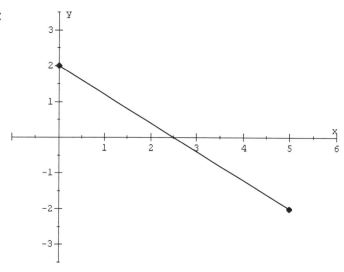

And then, the c-value looks to be around 2.5. In fact, it IS 2.5, but we don't need to figure that out to get the problem right. All that matters is that it is clearly LESS than 3. So the largest integer less than c is 2.

Once you know to make neat diagrams, the next thing to learn is how to deal with questions about slope.

EVERYTHING YOU EVER WANTED TO KNOW ABOUT SLOPE

We'll start with what you learn about slope in school: $slope = \dfrac{rise}{run}$ and so far, so good. No problem, yet.

The trouble begins when you turn this into algebra: $m = \dfrac{y_2 - y_1}{x_2 - x_1}$ and now it gets ugly. Let's try to straighten this out.

Slope Fact #1: You do NOT have to use the formula $m = \dfrac{y_2 - y_1}{x_2 - x_1}$ *!*

But if you insist on using it, please watch out for these three common traps:

i. The y-values go on top, even though x-values come first in the ordered pair (x,y).
If you get this backwards, your answer comes out as the inverse of the right answer.
In other words, if the right answer is 2/3, you will get 3/2.

ii. Be consistent: whichever point you take y_1 from you also take x_1 from.
If you switch, and take x_1 from the other point, you get the negative of the right answer.

iii. Be careful when you subtract negative numbers. The SAT knows that this is a common trouble spot, so they often put negative numbers in slope problems.

You can avoid all of these mistakes if you just learn the next fact.

Slope Fact #2: If you make a neat diagram, you can find the rise and run by counting boxes!

Just remember that as you go from left to right, if the line drops, you call that rise negative. So, for example:

Find the slope of the segment that connects the points (-3,3) and (1,2).

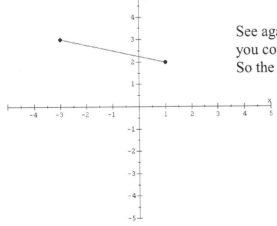

See again how a neat diagram makes it easy! And when you count the boxes, you see that the line falls 1 and runs 4. So the slope is −1/4. This answer is reasonable because…

141

Slope Fact #3: You should be able to look at a line and tell right away whether the slope is positive, negative or zero.

As you go from left to right…

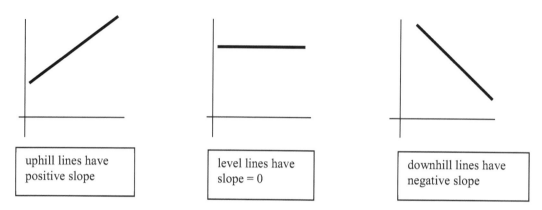

| uphill lines have positive slope | level lines have slope = 0 | downhill lines have negative slope |

Vertical lines have undefined slope, but I've never seen that fact on the SAT.

So in the problem on the last page, it makes sense that the answer was negative, since the line was going down hill. But that's not all. We can do a little better…

Slope Fact #4: You should also be able to tell if a slope is 1, more than 1 or less than 1.

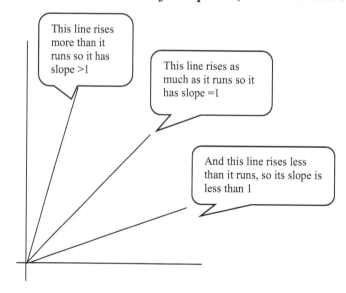

This also applies to downward sloping lines. So in that last example, since the line's drop was less than its run, we should be expecting the answer to be less negative than −1. And it was.

Slope Fact #5 and #6

Parallel lines have equal slopes.
Perpendicular lines have slopes that are the negative reciprocals of each other.

Practice Set # 15: Coordinate Geometry and Slope

1. What is the slope of the segment connecting the points (-2,2) and (2,0)?

a) –1/4   b) –1/2   c) 0   d) 2   e) 4

2. Line ℓ passes through the points (k,0) and (10,5). Its slope is greater than 2/3. If k is an integer, then the smallest possible value of k is:

a) 1   b) 2   c) 3   d) 4   e)5

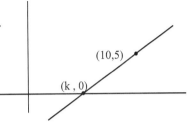

3. A circle of radius 6 is centered at the origin. It intersects the two coordinate axes at four points: A, B, C and D. If the x-coordinate of one of the four points is subtracted from the x-coordinate of another of the four points, the largest possible resulting difference is:

a) 3   b) –3   c) 6   d) 9   e) 12

4. An equilateral triangle, ABC lies with side AC on the x-axis as shown: If the length of each side is 3, what is the sum of the slopes of AB and BC?

a) 0   b) $3\sqrt{3}$ c) $6\sqrt{3}$ d) 6   e) undefined

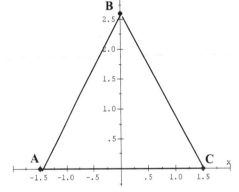

5. (A grid-in) Point A has coordinates (0, 2) and point B has coordinates (12, 6). If the midpoint of segment AB has coordinates (*a, b)* then $a - b =$?

6. The largest number of the sides of a parallelogram that can have positive slope is:
a) 0   b) 1   c) 2   d) 3   e) 4

Set #15: Answer Key

1. Draw a neat diagram, plot the points and then count the boxes to get the rise and the run:

As you can see, the line "falls" 2 and runs 4, so the slope is –2/4, which reduces to –1/2.
ANSWER: b

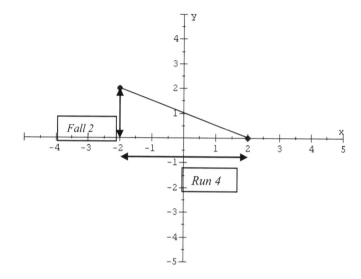

2. Let's try each answer choice. If k = 1, then the rise is 5 and the run is 9. But 5/9 is not greater than 2/3. If k = 2, then the rise is still 5, but now the run is 8. But 5/8 is also not greater than 2/3. If k = 3, then the rise is 5 and the run is 7. And 5/7 is greater than 2/3, so this is the one.
(By the way, if you are not sure which fraction is greater, use your calculator to change them both to decimals: 2/3 = .666…and 5/7 = .71428…)
ANSWER: c

3. Here's the picture:

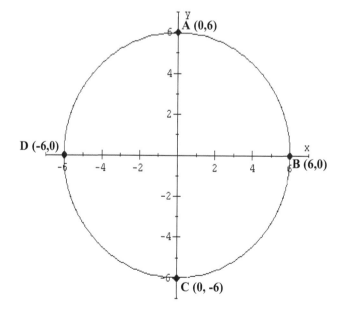

The coordinates of A, B, C and D are shown right on the diagram. (It didn't matter how we assigned the points to the letters, as long as we used the points where the axes met the circle.) The way to get the largest difference in x-coordinates is to take the biggest possible value, which is 6, and subtract from it the smallest possible value, which is –6. So the answer is 6 - -6 = 12.
ANSWER: e

4. Oh, this one is nasty. To find the slopes, you need the rise and the run. For each of the two segments, the run can be seen clearly on the diagram: it's 1.5 for each. But to find the rise for AB or the fall for BC, it looks like you'll need to use 30-60-90 triangle stuff, or at least the Pythagorean Theorem. But you don't. The two segments have the same run, as we said, but they have something else in common, too: however much segment AB rises, segment BC then falls. So the rise for one equals the fall for the other. This means the slopes will have the same value except AB's slope is positive and BC's slope is negative. So when you add them, you get zero.
ANSWER: 0

5. This one is not nasty. Just draw it neatly, find the midpoint, and use its coordinates as the *a* and *b* values…

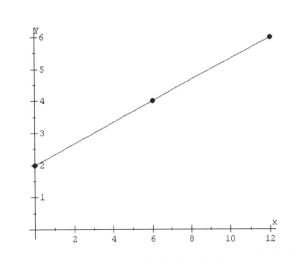

Here's how it should look:

The midpoint is (6,4). That means *a* = 6 and *b* = 4.

So the answer is *a* – *b* = 6 – 4 = 2.

ANSWER: 2

6. Well, let's look at some parallelograms and count how many of their sides have positive slope.

Here's one: Two of its sides have positive slope (they are going uphill).
Two of its sides have slope equal to zero (they are level).

So based on this first parallelogram, we'd have to say that the answer is 'c', because there are 2 sides with positive slope. But we are not going to just stop here.

Take a look at this next parallelogram:

Look closely—it IS a parallelogram. Both pairs of opposite sides are parallel. It just looks different than the first thing you think of when you picture a parallelogram. That's the trick. And if you'll notice, all 4 sides of this parallelogram have positive slope. **ANSWER: e**

More on Graphs: Lines and Parabolas

$y = mx + b$

The odds are that you already know how to graph a linear function. But if you need a quick review:

1. The 'b' value is the y-intercept. So start by graphing the point on the y-axis: (o, b).
2. The 'm' is the slope. So starting from your first point (o, b), count the rise and the run, going up and over (or down and over if the slope is negative). Then, connect your two points.

You can also just enter the equation on the "y=" menu of your graphing calculator. Then, press "Graph" and the calculator will do it for you. One advantage of doing it that way is that after you have the graph on your calculator, you can use the "Trace" feature to move along the line and see the points. That can be a lazy way to get an answer.

So, just to practice, try to graph the following three equations by hand and then, if you like, on a graphing calculator. The answers are on the next page.

1. $y = 2x + 3$

2. $y = 2x - 1$

3. $y = -\frac{1}{2} x$

BEFORE YOU CHECK YOUR ANSWERS...

Here are some things to notice:

Your first two graphs should be PARALLEL – they have the same slope.

Your last graph should be PERPENDICULAR to the first two – its slope is the negative reciprocal of their slopes.

If that's what your graphs look like then you probably did it right.

Here are the graphs:

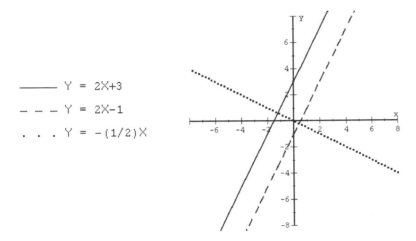

——— Y = 2X+3

– – – Y = 2X–1

. . . Y = –(1/2)X

And before we move on, one other thing to be ready for: sometimes, the SAT gives you a data set and then asks you to tell which equation best fits the data. All you have to do is draw your best guess for a line that fits the data and then use the slope and intercept to get the equation – or choose the equation which best matches. For example:

A bicycle manufacturer keeps track of the number of bicycles produced each week and the total weekly production cost. The data is graphed as shown. Which equation best models the cost as a function of the number of bicycles produced?

a) $c(x) = 15x$

b) $c(x) = .2x + 12$

c) $c(x) = .2x$

d) $c(x) = 15x + 12$

e) $c(x) = 10x + 15$

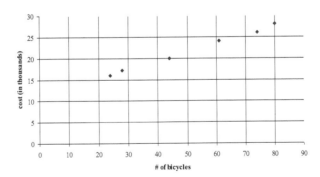

This is really easier than it looks. You have to draw a line that seems to go through the data points as best as you can. Then look at that line. First of all, it clearly has a y-intercept in the neighborhood of 12 so that narrows the answers down to choices 'b' or 'd'. (You don't have to be certain that it's exactly 12 -- it's definitely lower than 15 and more than zero.) Now find the slope of the line you have drawn. Would you say that it's closer to .2 or 15? I see. So the answer must be 'b'.

Parabolas

You barely need to know anything about parabolas on the SAT. In fact, I am going to pretend you've never heard of them. Just review the following:

1. The basic parabola is the graph of $y = x^2$:

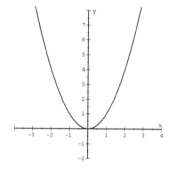

2. The rules of shifting, stretching and flipping all still apply. So, for example, if you shifted the basic parabola FORWARD 3 and UP 1, you would end up with:

$$y = (x\text{-}3)^2 + 1:$$

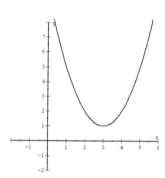

3. The general formula for a parabola is $y = ax^2 + bx + c$. So let's talk about a, b and c…

The 'a' value determines two things: when it is positive, the parabola opens up and when it's negative, the parabola opens down. And the higher the value of 'a', the steeper the sides.

The 'b' value – DON'T WORRY ABOUT IT. (Together, the 'a' and 'b' value determine the location of the vertex: x=-b/2a, but I have not seen this on the SAT.)

The 'c' value determines the y-intercept. This makes sense: when x=0, $y = a \cdot 0^2 + b \cdot 0 + c = c$.

These three rules will get you through the SAT. Also, if you know how to use your graphing calculator, these kinds of questions are the ones to use it on.

Practice Set # 16

1. Line ℓ has the equation $y=3x$. Line m is perpendicular to line ℓ and passes through the point $(0,6)$. If the equation of line m is $y=ax+b$, what is the value of $a \times b$?

2. At how many points does the parabola $y = (x-4)^2 + 4$ intersect the x-axis?

a) 0   b) 1   c) 2   d) 3   e) 4

3. Find the area of the triangular region enclosed by the x-axis, the y-axis and the graph of the line $y = -\dfrac{1}{4}x + 4$.

4. A line passes through the points $(2,1)$ and $(-1,7)$. Which of the following is the equation of a line that is parallel to that line?
      a) $y = 3x + 2$
      b) $y = -2x + 3$
      c) $y = 2x - 3$
      d) $y = -\frac{1}{2}x$
      e) $y = \frac{1}{2}x + 4$

5. A group of students went outside on one sunny late afternoon and measured the heights of a variety of objects and also the lengths of the objects' shadows. Then, they graphed their results as shown. Which of the following equations best models the relationship between shadow length, s and height, h?

      a) $s(h)=h+10$
      b) $s(h)=3h$
      c) $s(h)=10$
      d) $s(h)=10h$
      e) $s(h)=10/3$

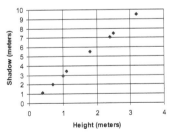

6. Given the line: $y = (\frac{1}{2a})x + 3k$, where a and k are non-zero constants, find the x-coordinate of the point where the line crosses the x-axis.

a) $x=-3k$ b) $x=-6ka$ c) $x=2a$ d) $x=2ka$ e) $x = \frac{-3}{2ka}$

Set #16: Answer Key

1. Since the new line is perpendicular to the original line, its slope, m, is the negative reciprocal of the original line. So a= -1/3. Then, since the y-intercept is (0,6), we also know that b=6. Then we multiply $-\frac{1}{3} \times 6 = -2$

Answer: -2

2. Either use your graphing calculator or just think: this is a basic parabola shifted 4 units to the right and 4 units up. So it never crosses the x-axis.
Answer: a

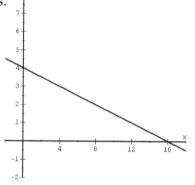

3. You have to start by drawing the graph:
Once you have the picture, it's easy to see
the base of the triangle is 16 and the height is 4.
This makes the area (16x4)/2 = 32.
Answer: 32

4. First, find the slope of the segment connecting the two points. I did it by drawing the diagram and then counting rise and run (actually, it fell and ran) to get a slope of -2. Then, since the lines are parallel, they have the same slope. So pick the only answer choice that also has a slope of -2.
Answer:b

5. Draw a line through the data points. You will see that the slope is around 3 and the y-intercept is close to the origin. There is only one choice that's close:
Answer:b

6. This is, of course, my favorite of these problems. We get to use the back door play. First I picked numbers for the variables: say a=3 and k=4. So now I have the equation: $y = \frac{1}{6}x + 12$ which I graph neatly. Then, by patiently counting back six and down 1, or by tracing on my graphing calculator, I find the line crosses the x-axis at x=-72. Yikes. But I am almost done. Now I go to the answer choices and plug in my numbers, and wow, I get a match with b and only with b!
ANSWER: b

Round 4 – Miscellaneous Fun Stuff

You may think that I am teasing about this being fun but I'm not. The topics in this section happen to be some of my favorite math subjects:

Counting problems – Let me NOT count the ways…

Probability – the least you need to know

Overlapping Categories and Venn Diagrams

What ARE these @!#&* symbols? …The made-up math on the SAT

It is possible that you have never learned this material before. These topics often fall between the cracks in a typical high school math program, which is a shame because these are interesting, useful topics and they are not hard to learn. If you ever have a chance to take a math elective with a title such as "discrete mathematics" or "probability and statistics" or "finite mathematics" I highly recommend it.

Of course, for our immediate purposes, it is completely irrelevant whether these are fun or not. The answer to the question "Why do we have to learn this?" is, as always: "Because it's on the SAT". But read this section with an open mind. You may actually enjoy yourself.

The Counting Principle: Let me NOT count the ways.

The Counting Principle appears on the SAT in many different forms. It can be applied to any of the following:

> Food, Clothing, Decorating combinations

> Arranging groups of people, tournaments, costumes, schedules

> Road map problems with multiple paths from Town A to Town B

> Number combinations

These situations don't seem to be related to each other, but the questions about them do have the following in common:

1. The questions typically ask how many ways there are to do something
2. When you try to list the possibilities, you soon realize that there are WAY too many to count.
3. If you know the Counting Principle, you can find the answer without counting.

We'll start with a very straightforward example:

Your favorite restaurant offers a combo-meal. You get to pick one each from a menu of 6 sandwiches, 4 side salads, 5 beverages, 10 desserts and 3 souvenir toys. You decide to eat at this restaurant once every day, ordering a sandwich, salad, beverage, dessert and toy every time, until you have had every possible combination. To the nearest whole number, how many years will it take you?

Do NOT attempt to list all of the combinations. Instead, learn the Counting Principle:

In any situation where you are faced with a series of decisions, keep asking yourself:

> ***"Now, how many choices do I have?"***

until the last decision has been made. Then, to find the overall number of combinations, you multiply together all the numbers of choices you had for each decision.

So in the example I have given you, you have to choose your sandwich from 6 choices, then your salad from 4 choices, your beverage from 5, your dessert from 10 and your toy from 3. And then you are done making decisions. So you multiply and find that there are

$6 \times 4 \times 5 \times 10 \times 3 = 3600$ combinations. And then we can divide by 365 days in a year and find that it would take just under 10 years to order every combination. That's a long time but don't be surprised. When you have lots of decisions, or lots of options, you get big numbers.

The example I just gave you is one of the easiest kinds of counting problems you'll see on an SAT. Many of the other varieties are a little harder to recognize and a little trickier to answer, as the next few examples will show.

The Counting Principle and Arranging Stuff:

Five friends, Allen, Bob, Cathy, Dave and Edward, are waiting in line for a movie. They take turns jumping ahead of each other, which changes the order of the line. How many different orders are possible?

Well, you can TRY to list them all. Good luck. Or, you can think:

Suppose I tell each person where to stand in line. I have five people and five places in line. So I'm going to have to make some decisions. In fact, I have to make a SERIES of decisions. Why, this looks like a job for...THE COUNTING PRINCIPLE!

So where do you want Allen to stand? Pick a spot and write his name.

_____ _____ _____ _____ _____

Ok, didn't you just make a decision? You decided to put Allen's name somewhere. How many choices did you have? _____ *

And now you have to make ANOTHER decision: where to put Bob. Go ahead and put his name somewhere. But again, the important question is: how many choices do you have this time? _____ **

And now you choose again for the next person, from how many choices? _____ ***

By now, I hope you get the idea: with each person, you have one fewer choice of spots than you did with the previous person. When you get to Edward, you will have only one choice: the last spot that's left.

Finally, you multiply your options: 5x4x3x2x1=120, and that's your answer. Aren't you glad you didn't try to list them all?

By the way, your calculator may have a button that does this for you in one step. It's an exclamation mark, and it's called the Factorial symbol. Try it and you'll see:

$$5! = 120$$

(But if you've never heard of this, or your calculator doesn't have this feature, just multiply the numbers the usual way.)

---

* You have 5 choices for the first person.
** Now you have only 4 choices, because one of them was already taken.
*** And now you only have 3 choices.

Here is another twist on the same theme:

Ryan is choosing his classes for the first four periods of the school day. The classes available are English, History, Geometry, French, Gym, Study Hall, Band, Chemistry and Photography. Each of these classes is available any of the first four periods, and he may not take any of them more than once in a day. How many different schedules are available to him?

Let's see. He has four choices to make. _____ _____ _____ _____
Can you fill in the numbers?
Try before you read on.

*   *   *

He has 9 options. Then 8. Then 7. Then 6. And that's his last decision. So its 9x8x7x6=3024 possibilities.

Notice that we did NOT keep multiplying 9x8x7x6x5x4x3x2x1. We only had 4 decisions to make. Then we stopped. That's what made this one different.

And what if he had been allowed to take the same class more than once each day? Think about it before you look below…*

One more twist…

ARRANGING STUFF WITH RESTRICTIONS:

A family of four children and their parents are sitting in a row of six seats at a theater. The management requires that one parent sits on each end. In how many ways can this family be seated?

Once again, you are faced with a series of decisions—six of them, to be exact:

_____   _____   _____   _____   _____   _____

Try to fill in the numbers yourself before looking at the next page.

_____

* It would be 9x9x9x9

Here are the numbers, with explanations:

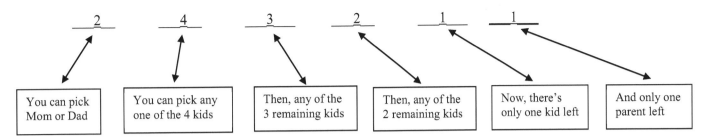

2	4	3	2	1	1
You can pick Mom or Dad	You can pick any one of the 4 kids	Then, any of the 3 remaining kids	Then, any of the 2 remaining kids	Now, there's only one kid left	And only one parent left

And so finally, you multiply 2x4x3x2x1x1 = 48 ways for them to sit.

*   *   *

This next example doesn't seem anything like the last one...but wait and see how it turns out.[*]

How many <u>even</u>, four digit numbers have a seven as the tens-digit? (For example: 3,576 is one such number.)

Why should you suspect that you could apply the counting principle? Well, the question is "How many?" and you can start by listing a few. But then you realize (I hope) that to write down some arbitrary 4-digit number, you have to make a series of decisions, one for each digit:

_____ _____ _____ _____

But there are some restrictions here, so think carefully, as you once again answer the question "Now, how many choices do I have?"

The answer is on the next page, but before you give up, here are some hints:

1. In general, the digits of a number can be 0,1,2,3,4,5,6,7,8,or 9.
2. But the thousands digit can't be 0 (or it wouldn't be a 4-digit number any more).
3. The tens digit must be 7.
4. The ones digit must be 0,2,4,6 or 8.

Pretty good hints, I think.

---

[*] I think that is why I particularly like this topic. A wide variety of seemingly unrelated problems can be solved by applying the same basic principle.

So were the hints good enough? Look at the answer and see:

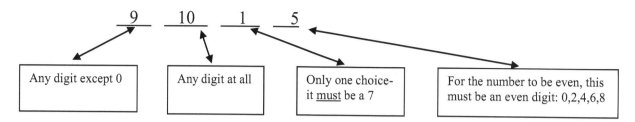

And then once again, we multiply the options to get the final answer:

9x10x1x5 = 450 even four-digit numbers with 7 in the tens-digit.

*   *   *

Ok, one more example, and once again, there will be a twist that makes it look different…

The map below shows the roads between towns A, B and C. Each road is marked with an arrow to show the direction of permitted travel on that road. Roads with a double arrow allow traffic to go in either direction.

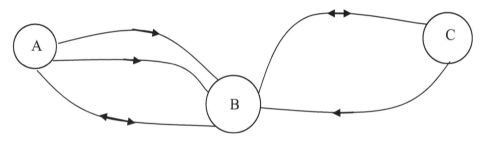

If you wish to drive from A to B to C, then back to B and finally back to A, how many different routes are possible?

Would you like a hint? You have to make FOUR decisions: how to go from A to B, from B to C, from C back to B and from B back to A. For each of those, think about how many options you have. Then multiply your answers. The answer is below.[*]

---

[*] It's 3x1x2x1=6 ways.

Practice Set # 17: Counting Problems

1. (Grid-in) How many 3-letter codes can be created using only the first 10 letters of the alphabet (a-j), with no letter used more than once? (So, for example, EJB and HCF would be allowed. But DDJ would not.)

2. (Grid-in) In how many orders can you arrange the letters A, B, C, D, and E if you must start with a vowel?

3. Patrick is completing a survey in which he is asked to name his favorite day of the week, his favorite month of the year and his favorite time of day – morning, afternoon, evening or night. How many different ways can he answer?

    a) 21   b) 23   c) 240   d) 288   e) 336

4. Every year, the Northern Conference winner plays the Southern Conference winner for the Rugby Cup. There is the same number of teams in each conference, and there are 64 possible match-ups for that final game. How many teams are in each conference?

    a) 4   b) 8   c) 16   d) 32   e) 64

5. How many even, 5-digit positive integers are there?

    a) 4500   b) 45000   c) 50000   d) 99999   e) 100000

6. (Grid-in) You are choosing your first period class and your second period class from a list of available classes. You cannot choose the same class twice. If there are 30 ways for you to make your schedule, how many classes are on the list? (You should count "1. Math, 2. French" as a different schedule than "1. French, 2. Math")

Set #17: Answer Key

1. You have 10 choices for the first letter of the code, followed by 9 choices for the second letter, and 8 choices for the third letter, giving you a total of 10 x 9 x 8 = 720 ways to make codes.
ANSWER: 720

2. You have 2 choices for the first letter (A or E) followed by 4 choices for the second letter, then 3, then 2, and then 1.
So there are 2 x 4 x 3 x 2 x 1 = 48 possible orders.
ANSWER: 48

3. Patrick has 7 choices for favorite day, 12 choices for favorite month and 4 choices for favorite time of day. So there are 7 x 12 x 4 = 336 ways for him to answer the survey.
ANSWER: e

4. You have to choose one from each conference. The number of possible match-ups is the number of teams in each conference, multiplied together. The numbers are the same, and when multiplied, the product is 64. You can try each answer choice, or just think: what's the square root of 64?
ANSWER: b

5. This is a deceptively difficult problem. To make up a 5-digit number, you have to choose each of the five digits. You have the following number of choices for each digit:

      <u>9</u>   <u>10</u>   <u>10</u>   <u>10</u>   <u>5</u>

Here's why: The first digit can be any digit EXCEPT 0.
                      The second digit can be any digit.
                      The third digit can be any digit.
                      The last digit must be 0, 2, 4, 6, or 8 for the number to be even.

Then, multiply those numbers: 9 x 10 x 10 x 10 x 5 = 45000.
ANSWER: b

6. Let's take a guess and see if it's right. Suppose there were 10 classes on the list. Then, you'd have 10 choices for your first class, followed by 9 choices for your second class. That makes 90 possibilities. But that's more than the 30 ways we actually have. So our guess was wrong—it was too high.

Next guess: how about 5? Then we'd have 5 choices, followed by 4 choices which makes 20 combinations…too low.

Next guess: how about 6? Then we'd have 6 choices, followed by 5 choices, which makes 30! We're done.
ANSWER: 30

Probability

The probability problems on the SAT are based on just a handful of basic concepts. Then, when they want to make the problem harder, once again they blend in algebra, and once again, we can avoid the algebra using trial and error or the Back Door play. As always, you are better off playing than you are using formal high school math. But first you have to know the concepts.

The Definition:

The probability of an event ("event" is the mathematical term for a thing that happens) is a ratio that compares the number of ways the event can happen to the total number of things that can happen. This is easier to understand if you look at a familiar example:

Suppose you are going to flip a coin and you want to know the probability of getting "heads". The answer is ½, because there is 1 way to get the thing that you want and 2 ways that the coin can land.

Or here's another: suppose you roll a die[*], hoping to get a 6. There are 6 things that can happen and 1 that you want, so the probability is 1/6.

This can all be summed up in an easy formula: $probability = \dfrac{desired}{possible}$.

A Warning:

Be careful not to confuse "Probability" and "Odds". The odds of an event are also expressed as a ratio, but this time it is the ratio of the number of ways of getting what you want to the number of ways of NOT getting what you want (rather than the total number of possibilities). So the odds of getting "heads" when you flip a coin are 1:1 and not 1:2. The SAT does not ask questions about odds.

So let's try a quick warm-up question, just to be sure you get the idea:

A letter is chosen at random from the 1st ten letters of the alphabet. What is the probability that the letter chosen will be a vowel?

Try it yourself before looking at the next page.

---

[*] There will not be any references to playing cards or dice on the SAT. There MAY be a reference to a cube with the numbers 1 – 6 printed on each of its sides.

Well, I hope you listed the 1ˢᵗ ten letters: A B C D E F G H I J

And I hope you recognize a vowel when you see one. In this list, that would be the A, E and I. So there are three of them. That makes the probability 3 out of 10 or 3/10.

Now try these next two. They are not any harder, but they are each designed to illustrate a conceptual point.

A cube has the integers 1 through 6 written on its faces (one on each face).
If the cube is rolled randomly, what is the probability that the number on the top is less than 10?

A letter is chosen at random from the word "FACETIOUS"*.
What is the probability that the letter chosen is also in the word "NYMPH"?

Do your answers surprise you? When you look at the first one, you might think, "Wait a minute. They are all less than 10. Is this a trick question?" It's not a trick. There are 6 numbers that you can get, and 6 of them are less than 10, so the probability of getting a number less than 10 is 6/6. Of course, 6/6 = 1. That's the conceptual point I am trying to make here:

When something MUST happen, it has a probability of 1. And 1 is the highest probability that anything can have.

Then, the next one is the other extreme. There are 9 letters in FACETIOUS. And none of them appear in the word NYMPH. So the probability is 0/9 or just plain 0.
And the conceptual point is:

When something CAN'T happen, it has probability of 0. And 0 is the lowest probability that anything can have.

And that's all you need to know to answer probability questions on the SAT. Let's look at a few together, and then I'll give you some for practice.

---

* An interesting word. I believe that it is the shortest word that contains all of the vowels a,e,i, o,u in order. I don't think they will ask you this on the SAT, but it's good to know this kind of thing.

A jar holds candies that are all either red, yellow, blue or green. There are the same number of blue candies and red candies. There are twice as many yellow candies as there are red candies and three times as many greens than yellows. If you choose one at random, what is the probability that it will be either blue or green?

a) 3/8   **b) ½**   **c) 3/5**   **d) 4/5**   **e) 7/10**

Before you read the solution, please try making up numbers that fit the problem…

OK, here goes. It says there are the same number of blue and red. I pick 10 each. Then, since there are twice as many yellow, I'll make that 20. Then there are three times as many greens as yellows, so they have to be 60. Well, that means there are a total of 10 + 10 + 20 + 60 = 100 candies. Of them, 10 are blue and 60 are green so there are 70 that I want. And that makes the probability 70/100, which reduces to 7/10, choice 'e'.

How about a nasty one:

The Riverwood High School student council has representatives from the freshman, sophomore, junior and senior classes. Each year, the chairperson is chosen at random from all the members of the council. This year, the probability would have been 1/2 that the chairperson would be a senior, but at the last minute, 2 sophomores resigned and 4 seniors were added to the council. This raised the probability of picking a senior to 2/3. How many students are on the council now?

a) 15   **b) 18**   **c) 24**   **d) 30**   **e) 36**

Well this is certainly an annoying algebra problem. But it is easy (well, easier, anyway) if you use trial and error.

Could there be 15 on the council? Then 10 of them (2/3 of 15) are seniors. And before we added 4 seniors, there were 6 seniors and 11 on the council. And before the sophomores quit, there were 2 more council members total, or 13. But that makes the seniors 6 out of 13, which is not ½. So 'a' is wrong.

Could there be 18 on the council? Then 12 of them (2/3 of 18) are seniors. And before we added 4 seniors, there were 8 seniors and 14 on the council. And before the 2 sophomores quit, there were a total of 16 students on the council. That makes 8 seniors out of 16 total, which is ½, which is correct!

The problem we just did is as hard as any probability problem I've ever seen on the SAT!

Problem Set #18: Probability

1. (A grid-in) Seven tiles with letters spell out the word "EQUINOX". The tiles are turned facedown, and one tile is selected at random. What is the probability that the letter chosen is one of the letters in the word "OXYGEN"?

Questions 2, 3 and 4 (all grid-ins) refer to the following:

The students in a class all either walk to school or take the bus, and they either go home right after school, or they stay late for activities. Some of the information has been entered in the chart shown, with some of the row and column sub-totals entered in the chart.

	Walkers	Bus Riders	Sub-total
Go Right Home	12		21
Stay Late		8	
Sub-total	19		

2. If a student is selected at random, what is the probability that the student stays late and then walks home?

3. If a student walks home, what is the probability that went right home?

4. A student is selected at random. What is the probability that he walked home OR stayed late?

5. Five different books are placed on a shelf in random order. What is the probability that the books happen to be in alphabetical order by title?

a) 1/5   b) 1/26   c) 5/26   d) 1/120   e) 1/625

6. (A grid-in) The midpoints of the sides of a right triangle are connected to form a smaller triangle which is the boundary of the shaded region. If a dart is thrown so that it hits the larger triangle, what is the probability that it strikes the <u>unshaded</u> region?

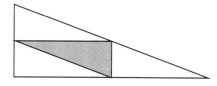

Set #18: Answer Key

1. There are seven tiles to choose from. And of the seven, 4 of them are letters that also appear in "OXYGEN" (the four are E, N, O, and X). So the probability is 4/7.
ANSWER: 4/7

2. First you have to complete the chart, making all totals come out right:

	Walkers	Bus Riders	Sub-total
Go Right Home	12	9	21
Stay Late	7	8	15
Sub-total	19	17	36

Then, you can see that there are a total of 36 students and there are 7 who stay late and walk home. So the probability of choosing one of them is 7/36.
ANSWER: 7/36

3. Still referring to the completed chart above, there are 19 students who walk home. Of them, 12 went right home. So the probability that a walker went right home is 12/19.
ANSWER: 12/19

4. Now we are choosing from all 36 students. Of those, we want all of the 19 walkers or the 8 late bus riders for a total of 27. This gives us a probability of 27/36 which we either reduce or grid in as a decimal.
ANSWER: ¾ or .75

5. There are 5 x 4 x 3 x 3 x 1 = 120 possible orders for these books (as you read about in the previous section on the Counting Principle). Of those, only 1 happens to be the right alphabetical order. So the probability of that happening randomly is 1/120.
ANSWER: d

6. There is actually a geometry theorem which can be used to show that the little triangle is ¼ of the area of the total triangle. You can probably tell just by looking. Either way, that means that the shaded region is ¾ of the total.
ANSWER: ¾

What ARE these @!#&* symbols? …The made-up math on the SAT

By now, I hope I have convinced you of the dangers of taking the SAT in an uninformed, clueless way. Students who do not learn the tricks behind the SAT do not score as well as they could have. In this section, I'll teach you how to deal with a type of problem that intimidates the typical unprepared student. But once you are prepared, these are harmless.

The problems look intimidating because they include mathematical symbols that seem unfamiliar. Like, for example:

Let a ~ b be defined for all integers by the expression a ~ b = 2a + b.
Then, 3 ~ (4 ~ 3) = ?

a) 10   **b) 13**   **c) 17**   **d) 23**   **e) 25**

Too many students omit this type of question because it preys on their insecurity:

I've never seen that symbol. I'm only in algebra-II. This must be pre-calculus or something. Or maybe the "honors" kids learn this stuff. But I'd better not mess with it.

Oh, come on now. At this point, you are too smart to be psyched out by the SAT. When you see a symbol that looks strange to you, there is actually a very simple explanation: THEY ARE MAKING IT UP! They love to do this. And if they are going to make up their own symbol, they have to tell you EXACTLY what it means. And if you were not so busy being freaked out by the strangeness of the symbol, you might have noticed the definition when they gave it to you.

These problems have a pattern that they all follow:

- In the first part of the problem, they introduce the symbol and they tell you what it means. As part of that, they sometimes include an example to illustrate what they have said.

- Then, in the second part of the problem, they ask you a question that will require you to use the new symbol.

Frequently, having made you learn a new symbol, they require you to <u>use it twice</u> on the same question. Also, they may ask two or three questions that all refer to the same symbol. In that case, watch out—they get harder as you go along.

Go back to the problem above and re-read it SLOWLY. Find where they tell you what the "~" means. Then stop. Think. Don't move on until you have understood what the symbol means.

Did you find it? It was **a ~ b = 2a + b**. In other words, they are telling you that you are going to see two numbers separated by a squiggle. And when you see that, it's the same thing as doubling the first number and then adding the second number. OK. We can do that. Now, we can move on to the rest of the question. The actual question requires you to use the symbol twice, and to know that you do what's inside the parentheses first.

So to calculate **3 ~ (4 ~ 3)**, first we calculate **(4 ~ 3)**, as follows: $2 \cdot 4 + 3 = 11$.

Then, we need to calculate $3 \sim 11$ which is $2 \cdot 3 + 11 = 6 + 11 = 17$. Was that so hard?

Now, we'll try three problems based on one new symbol:

Problems 11 – 13 are all based on the following definition:

For all real numbers, let ♦b be defined by ♦b = b^2 – 2b.

11. ♦8 - ♦6 =

a) 0   b) 12   c) 18   d) 24   e) 30

12. If ♦y = y and y > 0, then y =

a) 1   b) 3   c) 4   d) 4.5   e) 9

13. Which of the following expressions is equivalent to ♦ (x+2) ?

a) x^2
b) $x^2 + 2$
c) $x^2 + 2x$
d) $x^2 + 4x$
e) $x^2 + 2x + 2$

165

As I warned you, they got harder as you went along. In fact, the first one really just checks whether you understood the symbol: $\blacklozenge b = b^2 - 2b$. We are going to see a $\blacklozenge$ followed by a number. We are supposed to square the number, and then subtract twice that number. So the first problem just requires us to calculate:

$$(8^2 - 8 \cdot 2) - (6^2 - 6 \cdot 2) =$$
$$(64 - 16) - (36 - 12) =$$
$$(48) - (24) = 24$$

But the next one is a little harder. We are looking for a number that makes \$b the same as the number we started with. You COULD do this by algebra, starting with the equation:

$$b^2 - 2b = b$$

but that would be against the spirit of this book. Why use algebra when trial and error is so much easier? Let's try the answers one at a time, looking to see when we get the same number we started with:

a) $1^2 - 2 \cdot 1 = -1$. Nope
b) $3^2 - 2 \cdot 3 = 3$. Yep. And we're done.

And then we are up to the hardest of the three. But look at what we see: variables in the question, variables in the answer choices…it's time for the Back Door Play. Go back to the problem, make up a number for x, see what answer you get, put your number into the answer choices, see which one matches. I'll wait here…

Do you want me to do it? OK, I pick $x = 6$. Then $x + 2 = 8$. And $\blacklozenge 8 = 8^2 - 8 \cdot 2 = 48$.

And now, to the answer choices, still using $x = 6$:

a) $x^2 = 6^2 = 36$…no
b) $x^2 + 2 = 6^2 + 2 = 38$…no
c) $x^2 + 2x = 6^2 + 2 \cdot 6 = 36 + 12 = 48$…yes
d) $x^2 + 4x = 6^2 + 4 \cdot 6 = 36 + 24 = 60$…no
e) $x^2 + 2x + 2 = 6^2 + 2 \cdot 6 + 2 = 36 + 12 + 2 = 50$…no

Yet another victory for the Back Door play. (And yes, you could have done this one by formal algebra too—but why would you?)

I will give you more of these for practice, but once you understand these problems, they are easy to make up. Try it and see. Entertain your friends with problems that you wrote. Be the life of the party. It works for me.

Practice Set #19: Made-Up Symbols

Questions 1 – 3 refer to the following information:

Let [x,y;z] be defined for all integers x,y and z where xyz>0 by the equation $[x; y; z] = \dfrac{1}{x} + \dfrac{1}{y} - \dfrac{1}{z}$.

1. [1, ½ ;2] = ?

a) 1   b) 1 ½   c) 2   d) 2 ½   e) 3

2. Which of the following will always be equal to [a,b;c]?

a) [c,b;a]   b) [b,a;c]   c) [a,b;-c]   d) [a,b;1/c]   e) none of these

3. What is the value of: $\dfrac{1}{\left[\frac{1}{3}; \frac{1}{4}; \frac{1}{5}\right]}$?

a) 0   b) ½   c) 23/60   d) 60/23   e) 2

4. Let /w\ be defined as the <u>square</u> of the largest prime factor of w. Then /10\ - /36\ =?

a) -26   b) -16   c) 0   d) 2   e) 16

5. Let $\propto a$ be defined by $\propto a = (10 + a)/2$. Then $\propto 18 - \propto 8 = $?

a) $\propto 0$ b) $\propto 5$ c) $\propto 10$ d) $\propto 13$ e) $\propto 26$

6. (A Grid-in) Let *z be defined for all real numbers z by the equation *z = 2z - 4.
   If *(*(*x) = 12, what is the value of x?

Set #19: Answer Key

Before you attempt questions 1-3, you have to read slowly and make sure that you know what the symbol means. You are going to see 3 numbers, inside of brackets, separated by a comma and a semicolon. And you are supposed to invert each number (or divide 1 by each number, using your calculator), then add the first two results, and subtract the

third. How did I know that? Because that's what it said to do. Where? Where it said: $[x; y; z] = \dfrac{1}{x} + \dfrac{1}{y} - \dfrac{1}{z}$.

Oh. OK.

And now that we know what to do, we can try the questions:

1. Just use your calculator: $\dfrac{1}{1} + \dfrac{1}{\frac{1}{2}} - \dfrac{1}{2} = 2\dfrac{1}{2}$. You can enter this into your calculator exactly the way you see it.

Or, you can use a button on your calculator that inverts whatever you give it. Depending on your particular calculator, the button is labeled either "1/x" or "x⁻¹". Each calculator is different, so play around with it and see.
ANSWER: d

2. This would be hard if you didn't know the Back Door play. Make up numbers. I used a=3, b=4, c=5.

Then $[3,4;5] = \dfrac{1}{3} + \dfrac{1}{4} - \dfrac{1}{5} = \dfrac{23}{60} = .38333...$, as your calculator will tell you. Then, put those same numbers back

into each answer choice. You'll see that choice b) [b;a;c] is the only match. (It doesn't matter which order you add in. But
you can't change the order of subtraction.)
ANSWER: b

3. This one is hard if you don't know what to do when you see fractions in the denominator of fractions.

To begin, $\left[\frac{1}{3}; \frac{1}{4}; \frac{1}{5}\right] = \dfrac{1}{\frac{1}{3}} + \dfrac{1}{\frac{1}{4}} - \dfrac{1}{\frac{1}{5}}$. There are a number of ways to simplify this, but if you don't know them, then

your best bet is to use your calculator. Again, the sequence of buttons depends on your brand of calculator. But if

you do it right, you get 2. But be careful! We are not done. The question asks for $\dfrac{1}{\left[\frac{1}{3}; \frac{1}{4}; \frac{1}{5}\right]}$ which is $\dfrac{1}{2}$.

ANSWER: b

4. First let's make sure we know what the symbol means. They are going to put a number between those slashes. And we are supposed to find the largest prime factor and then we <u>square</u> that largest prime factor. So for /10\, first we find the largest prime factor of 10: it's 5. Then we find $5^2 = 25$. Now for 36, the largest prime factor is 3. And $3^2 = 9$. Finally, $25 - 9 = 16$.

Answer: e

5. For this symbol, we are to take the number, add it to 10 and then divide the sum by 2. But this problem has a nasty trap. Let's see what happens: we do 18+10=28 and 28/2 = 14. Then, 8 + 10=18 and 18/2=9. Now we have to subtract: you do $14 - 9 = 5$ and you are tempted to put choice b. BUT WAIT. Choice b is NOT 5. It's $\propto$ 5!!! There's a difference! $\propto 5 = (5+10)/2 = 7.5$ which is NOT what we want. So you have to try the other answer choices. When you try choice a, you'll see that $\propto 0 = (10+0)/2 = 5$ which IS what we wanted!

ANSWER: a

6. First step: read slowly, figure out what the symbol means. We are going to see a *, followed by a number. And we are supposed to double that number, and subtract 4. OK. We can do that. So now we are ready to continue…

$*(*(*x)) = 12$ means that they took some number, did the * thing to it, then took the result and did the * thing to that, and finally, took the result and one more time did the * thing. Of course, we have not forgotten that by "*", they mean "double and then subtract 4". So basically, we are looking for a number that you can double and subtract 4, then double your answer and again subtract 4, and then again, double and subtract 4, finally landing on the answer 12.

You can figure out the original number by writing and solving an equation—I won't try to stop you—but you can also use trial and error. For example, if we…

…start with 10. Double it. That's 20. Subtract 4. That's 16. Already too big…
…start with 5. Double it. That's 10. Subtract 4. That's 6. Now, double 6. That's 12. Subtract 4. That's 8. And one more time, double it. That's 16. Subtract 4. That's 12. Aha!

(You might think that I cheated, that I already knew 5 was the answer. After all, I wrote the problem. But I give you my word of honor: weeks went by between when I wrote the question and when I wrote the answer key. During that time, I forgot what the answer was. So, like you, I was just guessing. And I was happy and lucky to get the right answer on the second try.)

ANSWER: 5

Categories, Sets and Logic

In this section, we'll look at two kinds of problems that may seem unrelated. They are both about putting things into categories. In the bigger picture, these relate to set theory and logic -- topics that frequently are omitted from the high school curriculum.

1. Overlapping Categories

A baseball coach has a meeting with his infielders and outfielders. There are seven outfielders on the team and eight infielders. There were 12 players at the meeting and no one was absent. How many players are both infielders and outfielders?

I'll show you two different ways to answer this one. First, just by thinking about it, we realize that there must be SOME kids who play two positions because $7 + 8 = 15$ but there were only 12 at the meeting. So if you add the infielders and the outfielders, there must be some kids who you counted <u>twice</u>! That's the idea behind all of these types of problems: if you don't subtract the overlap, you end up counting things twice. In this case, the overlap must be the difference between the total of the separate categories ($7 + 8 = 15$) and the total number of players (12). So 3 kids must play both the infield and the outfield.

The second way to work this out is by using a Venn diagram:

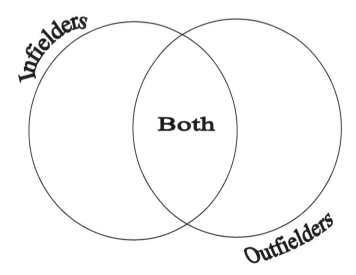

There have to be 7 players in the outfield circle, and 8 in the infield circle. But we can have only 12 players total, so we need to put some of the players in the overlapping section. You can actually make marks on the diagram, representing each player, moving them around until it comes out right. Your final diagram will look like the one on the next page.

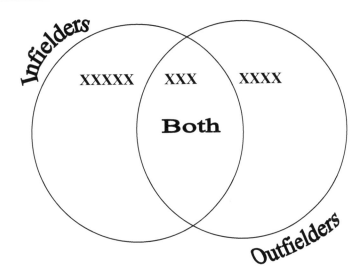

As you can see, to have 7 and 8 add up to 12, there must be 3 in the overlapping region.

*   *   *

2. A Common Logical Error

i.   **"If it rains, then my dog Ranger will get wet".**
ii. **"My dog Ranger is wet."**
iii. **"It is raining."**

Which of the following statements refutes the claim that if the first two statements are true, then the third statement must also be true?

a) **"No, because he could have just had a bath."**
b) **"No, because he might have stayed inside."**
c) **"No, because it's sunny outside today."**
d) **"No, because Ranger may not be a dog."**
e) **None of the above – the claim cannot be refuted because it's true.**

In general terms, the idea behind this question is that a conditional statements does not imply its converses. But what does that mean?

A conditional statement is a statement in the form "If …, then…".For example:

IF it rains, THEN my dog Ranger gets wet.

The converse of a conditional statement is what you get when you switch what comes after "if" with what comes after "then". So with our example, the converse would be:

IF my dog Ranger gets wet, THEN it rains.

The common mistake is thinking that if the first one is true, then so is the second one. But that is not the case. Let's take a closer look.

We are being asked to refute the claim that IF the first two statements are true, THEN the third one is also true. IF the first two statements are true, then we can assume two things. One is the conditional statement that if it rains, my dog will get wet. And the other is the fact that my dog is wet. We are supposed to accept that these two statements are true, and then we are trying to show that it would still be wrong to conclude that it must be raining.

And it WOULD be wrong. It says, "If it rains…" but it doesn't sat ONLY if it rains. There are lots of other ways for my dog to get wet. One of them is the occasional bath. So answer choice 'a' is the one that refutes the claim that it must be raining.

It's worth taking a look at the wrong answers b, c and d to understand why they are wrong. They are all different versions of the same mistake: arguing with the premises. No one is saying that my dog will get wet in the rain. No one is saying that my dog is wet. All they are claiming is that IF it is the case that if it rains, my dog gets wet, and IF it is the case that my dog is wet, THEN we can conclude that it is raining. Our goal is to show that their logic is faulty, not to disagree about the facts.

An easy way to remember that a true conditional statement does not always have a true converse is to think about the categories and sub-categories. Here is a true statement, but its converse is obviously false:

If you live in the United States, then you live in North America. (This is true.)
If you live in North America, then you live in the United States. (This is false.)

On the other hand…

If you start with a true conditional statement and then take its converse and make both parts negative, you end up with another true statement.[*] For example:

If you live in New Jersey, then you live in North America. (This is true.)
If you do NOT live in North America, then you do NOT live in New Jersey. (This one is true, too.)

So whenever you are lost in a logic problem, ask yourself what you would do if it were about states and countries.

---

[*] It's called the "contrapositive".

Practice Set #20: Categories, Sets and Logic

1. Seventeen students on a school bus bring their lunch to school in a bag. Nine kids on the bus buy their lunch at school. And three kids (unwisely) skip lunch altogether. If there are 25 kids on the bus, then...

a) 2 kids don't have bags
b) 4 kids bring lunch and buy lunch too
c) 4 kids missed the bus
d) 3 kids don't have money
e) 4 kids share their lunch money

2. The sign at the theater said: "If you have a ticket, enter through this door." Miles didn't have a ticket but he went through the door anyway. The manager stopped him and asked, "Why didn't you read the sign and follow the rule?" Did Miles break the rule?

a) Yes – if you don't have a ticket, you can't use the door.
b) Yes – if you go through the door, you have to have a ticket.
c) No – he didn't go through the door.
d) No – he had a ticket.
e) No – the rule doesn't say anything about him.

3. "All prime numbers greater than 2 are odd. N is odd and greater than 2. Therefore N is prime."
Which value can be used to show that the argument above is incorrect?

a) N = 2   b) N= 7   c) N=9   d) N= 29   e) none – the argument IS correct.

4. All 12 members of the Dance Club are also in the Theater League. All members of the Theater League are also members of the Performance Society, which has 40 members. If Q is the number of Theater League members who are NOT in the Dance Club, then the least possible value of Q is:

a) 0   b) 12   c) 28   d) 40   e) 52

5. (A Grid-in) A band of 30 musicians (it's a Big Band) is getting ready to catch a train. They have 22 suitcases and 14 instruments to carry. Every musician carries either a suitcase or an instrument, and some carry one of each. How many carry one of each?

6. Last year on every Monday in September (which has 30 days) Adam had pizza for lunch. Which of the following could be the number of times that Adam had pizza for lunch that month?
        I. 4
        II. 5
        III. 6

a) I only   b) II only   c) I or II   d) II or III   e) I, II or III

173

Set # 20: Answer Key

1. There are 25 kids on the bus. But 3 don't have lunch. So we have 22 lunch eaters. If 17 bring lunch and and 9 buy lunch, that adds up to 26 lunches for only 22 lunch eaters. So four of those hungry students are going to have to eat two lunches. You can see it in a diagram, too:

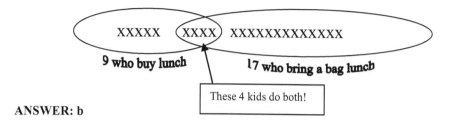

ANSWER: b

2. He did NOT break the rule. The rule is a conditional statement. It says what to do IF you have a ticket. Choice 'a' assumes that the negative (or inverse) of the rule also applies. Choice 'b' assumes that the converse (where you switch the order) also applies. But neither is correct. The rule says what to do if you DO have a ticket. It does not say anything about what to do if you do NOT have a ticket. So the answer is 'e'. By the way, 'c' and 'd' are both wrong for the same reason: they argue with the given information. You have to be able to assume that the given information is true. Otherwise, no question can ever be answered!
ANSWER: e

3. Look for an odd number, greater than 2, that is NOT prime. When you get to choice c, N=9, you've found it.
ANSWER: c

4. When you read this carefully, it seems almost silly. It is possible that the Theater League has as few as 12 members—the ones from the Dance Club. I know the Performance Society has 40 members, but other than the 12 from the Theater League, they could have 28 members from somewhere else. So it's possible that 0 members of the Theater League are not in the Dance Club. (It's also possible that ALL 40 of the members of the Performance Society come from the Theater League, in which case there would have to be 28 Theater Leaguers who were not in the Dance Club. But since they want the LEAST possible value of Q, this is not relevant. We already have the least value. It's zero.)
ANSWER: a

5. This is another version of the overlapping categories. We can make another diagram, or we can just think it out: They have 22 + 14 = 36 things to carry, but there are only 30 of them. So 6 of them will have to carry two things.
ANSWER: 6

6. You can spend time worrying about what day the month began on. But you don't need to know. Here's why: It's POSSIBLE that the month has 4 Mondays and that Adam had pizza on those 4 days. And it's possible that there are 5 Mondays. But here's the catch: It says that IF it was a MONDAY, THEN he had pizza. But it did NOT say that if it was not a Monday, then he did NOT have pizza. It could be that Adam has pizza every day! Or maybe just 4 Mondays and two Fridays. So 6 pizza lunches is definitely a possibility.
ANSWER: e

One Last Word: What to expect on test day

You've worked hard to get yourself prepared. You've read this book. You've worked through the exercises to learn the techniques. You've learned your game plan and you have taken practice tests to fine-tune your strategy. You can honestly say that you have done far more to prepare for the SAT than most other students, and you know more about what you are doing than they do. In short, you have given yourself a competitive advantage. Now, as the big day approaches, let's not blow it!

Once again, I have advice that seems almost too obvious to mention:

1. Get to sleep early the night before. Being sleepy costs you points.

2. Get up early, go for a walk, take a shower, and eat your normal breakfast. And while you eat, look over the Game Plan that you will follow for today's test. Then, skim through your best practice test to remind yourself of all the things you did right.

3. Bring snacks! 3½ hours is a long time. You can't eat during the test but you can during the breaks.

4. Take <u>every</u> break you are entitled to. The SAT's rules say that you are supposed to get a break after every hour of testing. (It says so on their web page.) **Do not let the proctors rush you past a break!** I've heard of proctors who say to the class something like, "You guys want a break or do you want to keep going?" If that happens, raise your hand and say that you have to go to the bathroom. Then go. Wash your face. Stretch. Move. Stay awake. And then come back, ready to attack the next section.

5. Follow your Game Plan! It is NOT just for taking practice tests. It's for the ACTUAL test as well.

6. Stay calm and go slowly. Try to <u>walk</u> your way through the test. This event is a marathon, not a sprint. (Or is it a basketball game? I forget.) Do NOT worry about finishing. Spend as much time as you need.

COMMON MENTAL TRAPS

While you are taking the test, you may find yourself worrying—it's been known to happen. It might help you to know that the following thoughts are common and can all be pretty much ignored:

"This is not going well."

Relax. It's going fine, and you are just worrying because everyone worries during the SAT. When you get a problem right, you forget it immediately. When you feel stumped, it sticks with you, so you think you are doing poorly. It's just a distracting waste of energy to worry about how you are doing while the test is still going on. Relax and let yourself play the game the way you have practiced.

"__This__ SAT is a hard one. The PSAT (or last SAT) was easier."

Again, just relax. It isn't harder or easier than the last one. Over the years, I have worked through dozens of SAT's, and boy can I tell you, they are ALL the same. That is one of the benefits of doing practice tests. It doesn't take many before you start to feel like an old pro.

"I can't believe how long it's been since I used the letter 'C'. And I have way too many 'E's. I must be doing something wrong.

Oh, please. You ARE doing something wrong. You're paying attention to the pattern of your answers. Cut that out right now. Just deal with each question as it comes and answer it as best you can. Then move on.

"I'm going too slowly. I had to skip some questions and I think I got a couple wrong. Now I need to go a little faster and answer a few more so I can catch up."

STOP. Take a deep breath. And slow down. You were just about to blow it. You were about to spiral out of control. NEVER rush. NEVER try to "catch up". First of all, you don't really know if you got a few wrong. Secondly, we EXPECT you to get some wrong – it's built into your Game Plan that you are going to miss a few. Thirdly, rushing and answering harder questions will only make things worse. What you really need to do is stick to the game plan and then go back to the ones you skipped. Don't forget: **The ones you skipped are easier than the ones that lie ahead!** If you keep your cool and stay in your Game Plan, you maintain your competitive edge.

Just For Teachers: How to use this book in your SAT course

If you are not a teacher, then this section will not interest you. There are no secret answers here, no hints that only the teacher gets to see. All this appendix has is plans for how to use this book if you are teaching an SAT course. Dull stuff, really. Nothing juicy, just teacher talk. Go on. Run along and play. Or go watch TV and let the grownups talk.

OK, the first thing I want to ask is that you read this book with an open mind. Math teachers, like stronger students, often resist the alternative techniques that I recommend in this book. "Isn't it easier just to use the algebraic method?" Well, of course YOU think it's easier—you're a math teacher! You look at the problem and you see the right equation. And you are fluent in your algebra.

For your students, it's just not like that. Most of them are going to be more comfortable, quicker and more successful when they adopt the non-algebraic techniques. And once you get hooked on the wise-guy way to do these problems, it becomes a fun game. When I do a practice SAT, my goal is to get through the entire test without doing ANY algebra. I'm disappointed when I have to solve an equation. It's more fun when you figure out a sneaky way – and you usually can.

Some of you may object on educational grounds: "If we teach students these tricks, then we are circumventing the educational purpose of the SAT!" All I can say is that the SAT does not have any educational purpose. It never did.[*] And, if you are teaching an SAT course, there is only one goal: helping students to raise their scores. Teaching them these non-traditional techniques is the fastest way that I know to reach that goal.

I teach the math section of a small SAT course in Red Bank, New Jersey. The course meets for 6 sessions, each 1½ hours long (that's just for the math). Other than this book, the students use *The Official SAT Study Guide*, not as a text, but for their homework. Each week, they are assigned another complete practice test to apply what I've taught. That way, they see immediate gratification and steady progress.

Q. *All of them?*

A. Well, nearly all of them. We do pretty well. It sometimes takes more than one try to get students to really slow down and be as patient as they need to be. But many kids get the idea right away and see their scores shoot up within just a couple of sessions.

The next page contains a sample syllabus for a typical 6-week session.

---

[*] There is an excellent book that I recommend if you are interested in understanding more about how the SAT came to be and just how awful a test it is: David Owen's *None of the Above*, Roman and Littlefield, 1999

SAMPLE SYLLABUS FOR A 6-SESSION COURSE

Session #	Lessons Covered	Notes and Comments
1	Lesson #1: It's About Time and Lesson #2 Trial and Error Lesson #3: The Back Door Play	It usually takes me 30 minutes to explain WHY to slow down. The basketball analogy really works. After that, students need to learn their Game Plan. Then, as we do the trial and error examples together, students start to see that this course is NOT what they expected or feared.
2	Lesson #4: The Grid-Ins	Only one lesson this week. But we also review the practice problems from Lesson #3 to make sure everyone has the Back Door Play completely understood. If there is time, we jump ahead to Functions from Algebra 2
3	Middle School Topics	Math Vocabulary Review Divisibility, Remainders and Pattern Problems Mean, Median and Mode (including Average Problems the easy way) Percents and Percent changes Ratio problems
4	Round 2 – Geometry Topics	All About Angles Four Useful Triangle Facts Pythagorean Theorem (and Special Right Triangles) Areas and especially Areas of Shaded Regions Coordinate Geometry and Slope the Easy way – just count the boxes!
5	Round 3 – Algebra 2	Finishing up functions, then graphs of lines and parabolas. Also, by now I hope to have convinced my students to use a Ti-89 and we spend time this week making sure that everyone knows how to use the solve menu (F2, Enter…)
6	Round 4 – Miscellaneous Fun Stuff that shows up on the SAT	Counting problems – Let me NOT count the ways… Probability – the least you need to know What ARE these @!#&* symbols? …The made-up math on the SAT Categories: Venn Diagrams and Logic One Last Word: What to expect on test day

NOTES

NOTES